Iditarod Sled Dog Tales and Tails

Terry Adkins, DVM
Jean Wise, RN

©2019 SimonSays, LLC. All rights reserved. No part of this publication may be reproduced, stored in a retrieval system, or transmitted, in any form or by any means, electronic, mechanical photocopying, recording, or otherwise, without the prior written permission of the copyright owner.

Edition 2

The Iditarod Trail Committee® holds registered trademarks for the following terms and language and are used by permission: Iditarod®, Iditarod Trail Committee®, Iditarod Trail Alaska®, Alaska where men are men and women win the Iditarod®, The Last Great Race, 1049 miles®, Anchorage to Nome®, and Mushing the Iditarod Trail®, Iditarod Days®, Junior Iditarod®.

The events and conversations in this book have been set down to the best of the author's ability, although some names and details have been changed to protect the privacy of individuals.

Cover photo of dogs, Fred (Astaire) and Roy (Rogers) from the movie star litter, Photo © Jeff Schultz/Schultzphoto.com

Newspaper credits:
Ravalli Republic (Gregg McConnell photographer), Hamilton, MT
The Frontiersman, Wasilla, AK
Anchorage Times, Anchorage, AK

Illustrations by Marina Koepke

Photos and images included without credit or reference are property of Terry Adkins.

ISBN: 978-0-9961755-1-7

sleddogstories@gmail.com

Table of Contents

The Ride 1
Evolution of the Iditarod Race 15
Tales of the Trail 33
   Tale 1: Joe Redington, Sr. 34
   Tale 2: The Trail 37
   Tale 3: After you, Ladies 42
   Tale 4: Physicality 48
   Tale 5: Feeding the Flock 51
   Tale 6: Sled change 56
   Tale 7: Lasting friendships 61
   Tale 8: Eating on the Trail 64
   Tale 9: Sleeping on the Trail 67
   Tale 10: Lesson in Humility 71
Tails of the Trail 73
   Tail 1: Oscar 75
   Tail 2: Chinook 79
   Tail 3: Patsy 81
   Tail 4: April 84
   Tail 5: Herbie 88
   Tail 6: Bony 90
   Tail 7: Oly 93
   Tail 8: Gladstone 98
   Tail 9: Bear 106
   Tail 10: Ranger 109
   Tail 11: Amigo 113

Preface

I am thankful for the many dogs who have blessed me in so many ways. In the 40-plus years I have been involved with sled dogs, I have seen advances in breeding and racing that continue to ignite passion for this sport. Sled dogs are the toughest animals on earth. Research has proven they have the ability to exert more energy per hour for longer hours at a time than human counterparts in the most elite athletic events including the Tour de France bike race and Olympic competitions. Racing or not, sled dogs are mans' best friends. The connection and trust between dog and musher are not exclusive to the trail. It is a relationship that is built in the kennel. After decades of time, I still love to train and work with the dogs I have. I enjoy seeing a young dog embrace the job while in harness or a young leader learn and complete commands. I revere the seasoned dogs I rely on to do their jobs impeccably and allow me to discard apprehension that we cannot handle any problem that may arise. It remains difficult to watch an older dog realize they cannot 'keep up' with the youngsters on the team. I reluctantly admit my aging body is unable to enjoy the maximum potential and capability of the dogs I have, but that does not dispel my desire to be with them. It is relaxing to watch my dogs play together in open runs while I sit in a chair amongst them.

I am thankful for my Iditarod experiences. It has been a great pleasure to watch the progression of mushing and this race. I have developed friendships with stellar individuals who share these thoughts and some of the same experiences. The Iditarod can be exhausting and miserable at times, but it can also be very fun. Despite the fun or misery, one cannot reach the burled arch of Nome in the company of his or her closest, canine friends without having the feeling of accomplishment that could enable the confidence to spit in a tiger's eye. Every year, I feel the call of the Iditarod. I appreciate the technology that is available surrounding the race. Through the use of GPS tracking and the internet, I am able to follow and applaud the up-and-coming Iditarod stars and how they strategically race.

I am thankful for the advances in canine veterinary medicine and general care guidelines for any dog-powered event because of the Iditarod race. On any given year, the Iditarod veterinary medical team is comprised of over 40 veterinarians, over 100 veterinary technicians, and countless volunteers from all over the world--quite different from the first year when the medical team was me, myself, and I. I believe the advances of improved dog care and training will continue because of the research that is generated from the Iditarod race. Each and every dog that runs the Iditarod race is required to have a thorough physical assessment by a veterinarian, a complete chemistry panel and blood count, and an electrocardiogram prior to participating. Studies are performed using that compiled data to propel advances in care. There is a veterinary team at each checkpoint of the race; each and every dog is assessed by this team upon arrival at the checkpoint. If a dog is "dropped" from the race, meaning the dog will no longer continue racing, the dog is immediately accepted by this medical team for assessment, care, intervention if needed, and observation until the dog can be safely flown to Anchorage where the musher's handler will assume care.

Lastly, I am thankful to live in the United States of America where we can freely participate in this type of life-style and event, as well as, thrive under the protection of our military forces. I am a United States Air Force veteran and it was because of my affiliation with the Air Force and being stationed in Alaska that founded my union with the Iditarod.

Terry O. Adkins, DVM, MPH, Lt. Col. USAF Retired

The Ride

Enjoy the Ride

Endurance dog mushers probably do not live longer than other people, but I think they definitely get more out of life than some folks. I have never met an endurance musher who was not awed by the splendor of the country and impressed by the elements. Nor have I met but a few who did not appreciate the bond they had with their dogs. Whether it is an illusion of long life, or in fact the realization of a long full life, I have enjoyed the ride.

"Kentucky is a wonderful place to be raised," I always say, and it is. Beautiful countrysides adorned with draws, creeks, and deciduous trees weave into the rolling hills which hold magnificent beauty. Yet, these landscapes are loaded with water-moccasin snakes, chiggers, and copperheads beneath the lush scenery. I was born and raised in Muhlenberg County, Kentucky in the 1940s. My parents were farmers of corn, tobacco, soy beans, hay, and our private food source. Our livestock included pigs, chickens, horses, crossbred cattle, and mules trained to plow the fields. My paternal grandparents lived with us in our two-bedroom house and also worked the farm. Dad enjoyed bird hunting and always had one or two hunting dogs that were either English Setters or English Pointers. Obviously much of our time was spent outdoors. Hunting, fishing, and giggin' frogs were only a few of the past-times. Electricity had not reached much of that area, including our farm. Coal mining was an active industry and we used coal for our primary lighting and heating source.

Early in life I decided I was going to be a veterinarian. Mom was very strict about scholastics and my educational conduct. The local school system made learning conducive, and the size of most grades was about 40 kids. By in large, most of the kids who I started the first-grade were the same kids I graduated with and have remained life-long friends.

After high school, I attended the University of Kentucky for two years and a summer. Auburn University in Alabama had a veterinary medicine program that accepted applicants into their program after three years of undergraduate study. I was accepted into Auburn's program and moved to Auburn, Alabama in 1963. Four years later, I graduated with my doctorate in veterinary medicine. During vet school, I married my first wife and joined the early commissioning program with the United States Air Force.

Upon graduation from veterinary school, orders sent us to Loring Air Force Base in Maine with my first assignment as the base veterinarian. Our oldest son was born there. I completed the USAF assignment which spanned two years. Afterwards, we returned to Ohio County, Kentucky where I operated a satellite program for three veterinarians. Acting as a sole veterinarian in a rural, ag-based community in those days required long hours and constant time on-call. One day after vaccinating and castrating a herd of Charolais calves, a friend I knew in the Air Force called. He happened to be in charge of assignments and asked, "Why don't you come back to the Air Force?" Covered in cow manure and bruises, that was a good and logical question.

"Where will you send me?" I asked.

He provided three options I did not like then concluded, "Where do you want to go?"

"Alaska."

Three days later I received a call, "You're going to Elmendorf, Alaska."

Base veterinarian at Elmendorf Air Force Base in the early 70s was an exceptional assignment. Outdoor life in Alaska took anything I had ever known to a whole new level. I experienced my first, true sled dog ride in Alaska with a man named Lloyd Haessler in 1971. Lloyd and his wife, Lil, owned a kennel named Lloyd's Lead Dogs. The job on the base was interesting with plenty of variety and provided experiences all over Alaska when flying to outlying areas for site inspections.

A year or so after being stationed there, I received a call from Fort Yukon Air Force Base and was made aware that remnants of an Air Force sled dog team were in need of a new home. The team had been assembled to compete with the U.S. Army's team. A well-known dog driver was asked to represent the Air Force in the race. The competition resulted in a debacle for the Air Force team when a female husky in heat was placed in lead. Rumor had it the female stopped soon after leaving the starting line which caused the team to ball up and a huge fight erupted amongst the dogs. The Air Force general was embarrassed and sent the team to Fort Yukon. Apparently, the team had been there for a couple of years and resources had been exhausted to provide care for them.

I responded to their request by offering the security police, the nurse's squadron, and anyone else I could think of who might want a dog team. No one was interested. Finally, a Master Sargent who worked with me said, "Let's take them!" "Let's" meant the Veterinary Corps. I called a meeting with our entire office staff; and members of the staff were excited to get involved with the dogs.

I flew to Fort Yukon to do a site inspection and picked up the sled dog team. After my inspection, the troops stationed there broke out a bottle of Old Grand-Dad bourbon and poured it in tea glasses to celebrate ridding the sled dog team from Fort Yukon. The following day I returned to Elmendorf with a headache, seven dogs, a broken sled and an assortment of chewed harnesses. One dog was overwhelmed with arthritic pain and debility; after medication and care were ineffective to alleviate suffering, I had to euthanize him. Another dog bit one of my airmen and was subsequently euthanized due to the uncorrectable and unpredictable aggressive tendencies. I later visited the dog pounds of Elmendorf, Fort Richardson, and Anchorage. The visits provided the acquisition of about 40 dogs which we started to train at local races. It was at those local races where I met Joe Redington, Sr.

During the same time period, Joe Redington, Sr. had been working with a local historian, Dorothy Page, to recreate the passage and usage of the Iditarod Trail that spanned across Alaska. Originally, the trail was utilized by Native tribes but later constructed for access and transport of supplies during the Iditarod gold strikes. A portion of the trail was used for the renowned Serum Run, which saved the people of Nome from a diphtheria outbreak in the 1920s. Commencement of using airplanes and snow machines was gradually ending the heritage and culture surrounding Alaska's sled dogs and use of the Iditarod Trail. Joe with his wife, Vi, teamed with Dorothy Page to assemble an event to reintroduce dog teams from coast to coast of Alaska. They quickly sought and surrounded themselves with people who liked the idea and were willing to help such as: Dan Seavey, Dick Mackey, Dave Olson, Dick Tozier, Ed Carney, Al Hibbard, Rod Perry to name only a few.

In 1973, Joe Sr. asked me to go along as the veterinarian for the first Iditarod race. I think I was the only sucker he could find. Joe's approach when he asked you to do something was always convincing and never really a question. He had a way of making a race across some of the most rugged, wilderness trail with unforgiving elements known to man seem like a good idea…even though the trail, for years, had been unmaintained, overgrown, and, in some places, impassable. Joe had befriended a general from the Army. Joe requested his general friend to inquire the possibility of relinquishing the base veterinarian for the Iditarod Trail Race. After Joe wrote a letter to the base commanding officer, the Army general may have spoken to the Air Force general who commanded my superior officer to allow permissive temporary duty, which allowed me to go.

Dr. Terry Adkins/Jean Wise

IDITAROD TRAIL
International Championship Sled Dog Race
Anchorage to Nome March 3, 1973

1000 MILES-$50,000.00

Iditarod 1000　　　　　　　February 5, 1973　　　　　Iditarod Trail Committee
Committee　　　　　　　　　　　　　　　　　　　　　　　　Box 6108
Honorary Members　　　　　　　　　　　　　　　　　Anchorage, Alaska 99502

Governor William A. Egan
Lt. Governor H. A. Boucher
U.S. Senator Mike Gravel
U.S. Senator Ted Stevens
Sen. or Willie Hensley
May r Robert Renshaw
Mayor John R. Roderick
Mayor George M. Sullivan
Vi. e Bartlett
Al. n O. Bramstedt
Ed h Bullock
Ali o B. Gregory
Br ce Kendall
M. R. Marston
Ho ard W. Pollock
El er Rasmu son
Do Wright
John M. Asplund
Walter J. Hickel
Charles B. Towill

Major General Donvan H. Smith
Alaskan Air Command
Elmendorf AFB, Alaska

Dear General Smith,

As I am sure you have heard by now, March 3rd will begin the longest and most physically gruelling sled dog race ever held. I refer to the planned 1,000 mile Anchorage to Nome Iditarod Trail International Championship Sled Dog Race.

The Iditarod Trail Committee needs your help. We expect over 1,500 dogs to make the run to Nome. Needless to say, medical attention for the sled dogs will be a critical need.

I am writing to request the assistance of Captain Terry O. Adkins, Chief of Veterinary Services at Elmendorf. Captain Adkins can provide an invaluable service in the care of these animals.

We hope that we can rely on your help by allowing Captain Adkins to provide whatever training and care for the sled dogs that he is able.

Your assistance in this matter will be greatly appreciated.

Sincerely,

Joe Redington, Sr.
Chairman
Iditarod Trail Committee

During the starting day of the Iditarod Trail Race, I examined each dog of the 40 dog teams which were prepared to race. I disqualified one dog from the group due to an injury. One entire team was disqualified because of several tangles while leaving the starting line. All of the mushers were men. The majority of the dogs were brawny and densely-coated working dogs that happened to have been in some races. My education was just beginning; nothing in the curricula I had ever learned involved anything to do with what I was about to see. They were off. The Iditarod Trail Sled Dog Race from Anchorage to Nome was born!

The racers were sledding on the trail while I was flown in a bush plane from checkpoint to checkpoint to provide care and examination for the dog teams. Foot problems in the dogs were common. The only thing I had to put on some feet was a product called Kopertox®. Kopertox® was originally designed for foot rot in cattle. It left a lot of green tracks in the snow after an application. Dan Seavey used a mixture of Neatsfoot oil mixed with pine tar on his dogs' feet; he said it was an old trappers' recipe and it seemed to help protect the feet. Booties were not readily marketed at that time and few booties were used on the dogs. Predominately, the Native mushers were the only mushers using booties, which were made from sealskin.

Stress diarrhea and dehydration were common ailments in the teams. A commercial dog food company donated bags of dog food that some of the mushers used. When the dogs were trained using meats as their main diet prior to the race, diarrhea ensued due to the switch. The trail to Nome was unfortunately littered with excrement due to the stomach upset which exemplified the importance to "race them like you train them."

My medical background was not exclusively utilized on the dogs. Tom Mercer and Joe Redington, Sr. felt the sting of my suture needle for various maladies. The remoteness and limitation of resources the trail passed were ineffable. Hundreds of miles passed without any medical personnel available.

Joe Redington, Sr. flew me to the first couple of checkpoints. He liked to fly at tree-top level to enable a good view of the teams below us. I was more worried about hitting one of the trees than watching the teams. At one point of the trip, Joe began to fumble around in the plane and suddenly presented a pair of false teeth that he stuffed in a bag of dog food, "These are Rayme's teeth. He forgot them. I don't know why he needs them. All he took for food was a dozen hard-boiled eggs. Anyway, try to hit him with this sack when we fly over him." Acting as the bombardier, I launched the bag of dog food toward the moving dog team below then resumed gripping the seat while we skirted tree tops.

After reaching Susitna Station, Art Peterson piloted me for the remainder of the race. He was a very fine pilot and delivered me to and from checkpoints, many times, retracing previous checkpoints as the teams dispersed between the front-runners and the trailers. Art and I did well until we flew into white-out conditions leaving White Mountain approximately 80 miles from the finish. Everything was fine then suddenly, there was no visibility. Art asked, "Doc, can you see the pucker brush?"

"Yeah, it's about four feet below us!" I replied.

"Keep your eye on it while I try to turn this thing around," he instructed.

We returned to White Mountain, spent the night, and attempted to get to Nome by flying around the coast the next day. We made it as far as Cape Nome. Art radioed Nome. We were told there was an in-air emergency and further directed to Cape Nome and hold there. After we heard the tower personnel instruct two more planes to do the same, Art asked me if I had any objections to go to Nome over the dog trail. I told him I did not. To avoid the hold at Cape Nome, he landed the plane on the trail then taxied all the way to Nome on the sea ice. We parked the plane and climbed the bank onto Front Street. What an experience!

Dick Wilmarth had already crossed the finish line and won the race with his team. Twelve more days elapsed for all of the racers to reach the finish line. I was there and checked all of the dogs of each team. In total, I spent 35 days on leave to participate as the veterinarian for the first running of the Iditarod Trail Sled Dog Race.

I compiled my statistics and findings from the race including recommendations. The closing remarks of my synopsis were, "I will recommend that the race be held next year with certain modifications. I feel this type race will stimulate renewed interest in breeding back the endurance type of sled dog in Alaska. ...the Alaskan Sled Dog is an outstanding specimen and very worthwhile."

The following year I entered the Iditarod Trail Race with our team of 'Pound Hounds' the Air Force staff and I trained. I thought it would be easier to run the race than to work as the vet. Three veterinarians from the Army replaced me as the medical team for the dogs. Twelve dogs and I left Anchorage for our trek on the Iditarod Trail. Totally unprepared, yet I did not know the difference. The pair of wool pants from Sears with elastic bottoms would be laughable in this day and age, but that is what I wore. There was no ruff on the parka I wore. My sled bag was a couple of military-issued duffle bags that I crammed full and tied onto my sled. My sponsor, the Air Force, and I made no

Dr. Terry Adkins/Jean Wise

provisions for dropping dogs. Therefore, the twelve dogs I started in Anchorage finished in Nome with me. Essentially, it was an extraordinary training experience. The race paid the first 20 places, and we made it in the money with a 19th place finish. The plan was the 1974 race would be my only attempt over the Iditarod Trail, however I received an unimaginable gift of encouragement which launched a career--and it was not the pay-out.

```
RECEIPT    Date 8 April 19 74    4590
Received From Dr. Atkins
Address
                                           Dollars $232.50
For Iditarod winnings

ACCOUNT          HOW PAID
AMT. OF          CASH
ACCOUNT
AMT. PAID        CHECK    ✓
BALANCE          MONEY          By Via Derbonne
DUE              ORDER
```

Orders from the Air Force stationed me and my family to Mountain Home, Idaho and I was not able to participate in the 1975 running of the race although I went to Nome and worked at the finish line as a veterinarian. Late that year I enrolled in a Master's program from the University of Minnesota and we moved to Anoka, Minnesota. I was able to continue training dogs and raced the 1976 and '77 Iditarods. Kenny Hess traveled with my family and me while he helped handle and train the dogs. During the 1977 run, I took blood samples from my dog team and compiled data to complete my thesis on 'Creatinine Phosphokinase Levels in Racing Sled Dogs.' The other thesis I provided for my Master's degree completion, 'Chlamydia in Wild Mallards of Minnesota', obviously did not need an Iditarod run in order to write.

After graduation of a Masters in Public Health degree, we were stationed at F.E. Warren AFB in Cheyenne, WY where I was assigned as base veterinarian. My second son was born there. I continued running the Iditarod and building my kennel.

Orders were issued after a four-year tour in Cheyenne. My first marriage ended in divorce and I was sent to Malmstrom, AFB in Great Falls, MT. I was assigned the base veterinarian at Malmstrom. One of the ladies who had previously worked in my office introduced me to her sister, a nurse in the Air Force who I later married. We had my third son in 1983. Also that year, the Air Force relocated the veterinary programs, which discontinued the one at Malmstrom. Consequently, I was assigned the Environmental Health Officer for the base and worked that assignment until my Air Force retirement in 1988.

I continued running Iditarod until 1994 then announced my retirement from Iditarod. The late 1990s and early 2000s, I assisted a few individuals to run Iditarod and leased them my dogs while they trained from my house.

In addition to running Iditarod in the early 80s, I was fortunate to meet Dr. David Kronfeld at an American Veterinarian Medical Association convention. Dr. Kronfeld had a terrific mind in regard to dog nutrition and research; he had teamed with Alpo®. Alpo® sponsored my team for a couple years in the 80s. During the early 90s, the National® Dog Food sponsored me and my dog team in exchange for assistance to formulate dog food and supplemental products. A decade thereafter, I had the opportunity to work with Dr. Rob Gillette and the Auburn University Sports Medicine program to assess and devise solutions for foot issues in the military's working Improvised Explosive Device (IED) dogs. The impressive intelligence, capability, and constitution of our military dogs are indescribable.

The International Sled Dog Veterinarian Medical Association (ISDVMA), founded in the late 1990s, is an organization that compiles, provides, and encourages education of veterinarians, mushers, and handlers in all aspects of sled dog welfare and the supportive treatment of sled dogs. Veterinarians from all over the world are able to participate and include research and data from their home countries referencing any aspect of dog-powered sports and events. The first meeting was held in Helena, MT and I was able to attend and have continued my membership since that time. This association and its data coordination are valued assets to safely propel advances in the sled dog world.

In 2004, I donned the #1 Iditarod Trail Race bib and was named the honorary musher for that year's race. What a privilege! It was an exhilarating ride through Anchorage to be the first team out for the ceremonial run. Unfortunately, I later heard rumors of my death, because it not uncommon for a deceased person to receive the award.

My oldest son ran his rookie Iditarod race in 2010. My other sons met us at the start in Anchorage for support. Days later, my granddaughter and I stepped off a plane in Nome to meet my son and the dogs at the finish. He had a good trip across Alaska. We were able to stay with terrific friends who live in Nome and remembered my son as a boy. Our time there was nostalgic; there's no place like Nome!

Wyoming hosts a stage race every winter; it is called the Pedigree® Stage Stop Sled Dog Race. Stage racing is a much different type of racing compared to a distance event, like Iditarod. The race extends over a week's time, a 14-dog pool is allowed in each musher's team yet only 10 dogs or less are allowed to run per day. Every day of the race travels to a different location/town in Wyoming, Idaho, and some years Montana and Utah. The mountain towns welcome the mushers and their teams with Western hospitality and fun. I served as the race marshal for that event from 2014-2018 and it is truly remarkable. The dogs competing are setting new records for speeds at extended distances. Even though they do not run on a continuous format like the Iditarod race, they are capable at maintaining higher speeds for multiple days at a time.

My last trip to Alaska and the Iditarod race was in 2016. I was honored to receive the Joe Redington Founder's Award at Iditarod's pre-race banquet. During my time there, I was able to connect with many of my longtime friends who pioneered this event. Many of these individuals continue to actively support the race; their span of involvement is colossal. The ceremonial start delivered the unquenchable excitement for the dogs, mushers, and spectators. The build, movement, and conformation of today's Iditarod dogs were captivating traits to observe as the dogs passed through the starting chute and down the trail. I returned to Montana knowing I am currently blessed with some of the best dogs I have ever owned and would love one more race.

Evolution of the Iditarod Race

Then and Now

Progress of the Iditarod Trail Sled Dog Race has been remarkable at the very least. Iditarod was once measured by weeks; now it is days. As noted earlier, I was allowed 35 days of permissive leave to perform veterinary care to the teams during the initial run. Mushers traveled during the day and camped at night. There were no groomers. The race was not very well-known and the trail was minimally open due to overgrowth, so snow machines were not accessing the trail, either. If there was heavy snow during any given night, the trail would be snowed-in by morning which meant the dog-teams would have to break trail for miles. Today's race has more snowmobile traffic to pack the snow into a trail and groomers are available so the trail it set-up nicely. Certainly, storms can blow-out a trail, but most areas have a firm base set for a trail.

In 1973, the pilot and I dropped dog food from the air above the teams at Poorman, a community in Alaska's Interior, while we watched the racers snowshoeing in front of their dog teams. In 1974 when I was competing and after a heavy snow, we were negotiating a section of the Yukon River; Tim White and I snowshoed in front of our teams from Galena to Last Chance. It took the entire day to cover 18 miles. We spent hours snowshoeing in front of teams with patient dogs behind us. In retrospect, our dog teams were impressively levelheaded during the waiting and wading through unbroken trail.

Throughout the 70s, the trail remained extreme. Trail marking was a challenging feat. Many miles from Knik, the trail was marked by axslashes on trees. For the remainder of the trail, trail markers were spruce boughs rammed into the snow and scantily placed. Gusts of wind easily blew these spruce boughs to the ground leaving the trail unmarked. After a couple of years, the Iditarod Trail Committee used a tri-pod system to mark. The current standard has red paint and reflective tape erected with wooden stakes that can be seen a quarter mile away with a good headlight.

Dr. Terry Adkins/Jean Wise

[1]

Good headlights with reliable, polar-tolerant power sources had not been invented. We had large flashlights powered by D-cell batteries that were cumbersome and relatively ineffective in comparison to the use of lithium battery and LED lights. During my 1974 run while traveling the coast (later in the day than I had planned) I crouched down on the ice with my medical pen light in an attempt to find scratch marks on the ice made from previous sled teams to ascertain I was still on course. Years passed and we upgraded headlights with cords running from the light to a large battery pack that was secured under our parka. Today's racer now has powerful headlights that use as little as 3 AA Lithium batteries that are capable of hours of travel in sub-zero temperatures.

---

[1] Note the tripod next to the trail on the right; this example was taken on the Bering Sea coast.

Safety was an issue. The initial races sent dog teams to run parallel with highway traffic on the trip away from Anchorage to Knik. The teams demonstrated extreme trust in the musher as well as discipline to remain unnerved by the traffic. Some of these dog teams were born and raised in the 'bush' of Alaska. Vehicles, noise, and urban life was something they had never seen. Some mushers came from places so isolated that their dogs had never seen another dog team.

2

Dog booties were rare. Native Alaskans and the first-generation homesteaders had variations of dog booties; the Eskimos handstitched seal-skin booties. It did not take long for all mushers to focus care and protection to maintain healthy feet for their canine athletes. Many of us

---

[2] Pictured is a team running next to the highway on the Knik River Bridge which is shortly after the start of the race.

created our own version of a bootie including the use of denim, leather, nylon, and fleece to name a few of the materials. Equally evolutionary were the fasteners to keep the bootie on the dogs' paws. Shoe strings, leather straps, electric tape were some of the materials we tried. I have been reduced to using my teeth to remove the frozen, feces-laden tape from a bootie in order to get the bootie off a dog's foot. Velcro®, and more specifically elastic Velcro®, was the jackpot of all fastening woes. Industry standard for bootie construction is now Cordura® fabric with a sewn-on Velcro® fastener—much, much simpler. And booties are now mandatory: "Eight booties for each dog in the sled or in use."[3]

The heavily-constructed sleds used for trap-lines and wilderness travel converted to racing sleds for the initial Iditarods. The runners were made of steel or wood and the frame constructed of wood with metal brakes. Obviously, those materials added weight and when marred, scratched, or wet, created a great deal of drag for the dogs to pull. Study of plastics, light-weight metals and alloys drove invention of quick-change runners, Rex™ runners, air-craft grade aluminum, titanium, carbon fiber, fiberglass, Kevlar® that are used for various parts of sled design and manufacturing in today's race.

The Alaskan Husky was not then, and is not now, an AKC registered dog. An Alaskan Husky is a Northern-breed dog crossed with some other type of dog depending on what type of pulling or racing is desired. Alaskan Huskies are noted by the build and mindset representing various regions of Alaska; breeding focuses on qualities of strength and performance. As the race conditions improved, racers shifted to breeding a faster, less-burly dog. The cross-breeding also integrated a more easily trainable dog. Old-school dogs were usually stoic and, many times, stubborn with a strong pack orientation. Recent years have witnessed a resurgence of Siberian Husky teams entered and many breeders are striving to recover the working Siberian lines without the anomalies that many pure-bred dogs have. It is a nice addition for

---

[3] © Iditarod Trail Committee (2016, Oct) Iditarod Trail International Sled Dog Race Official Rules 2017. Retrieved from Iditarod.com/race/rules/Rule 16

spectators who expect to see the fuzzy, pretty Siberian Husky instead of our diverse, scrappy-looking Alaskan Huskies. No matter the breed, then and now, the dogs will only do what they have been conditioned and trained to do.

Technology is wonderful. After my first completion of Iditarod in 1974, I was greeted at the finish line with a telegram--yes, a telegram. The logistics for the race officials in the first 20 years of Iditarod racing relied on telegrams, ticker tape, Ham radios, and telephone, if fortunate to have a telephone. It is hard to imagine how they did it.

```
                    1974 MAR 28  AM 9 42


V
02003 ANCHORAGE ALASKA 15 03-28 1020A ADT
PMS DR TERRY O ADMKINS AND TEAM CARE IDITAROD RACE
NOME
BT
CONGRATULATIONS ON YOUR EXPEDITION TO NOME
MARK AND HOLLY LESKO
```

The internet and GPS tracking opened a whole new format for monitoring and studying race strategy, not to mention, it created a whole new availability for the spectator. From the warmth of my Montana home, I love to awaken at 3 a.m. on any given day during the second week of March and know how many racers are in and out of first 400 miles of checkpoints on the Iditarod Trail Sled Dog Race.

Dr. Terry Adkins/Jean Wise

Coordination of details from the Iditarod Trail Committee delivers amazingly frequent updates during the race when racers disperse over a 250-mile span of the trail. Technology has delivered to fans, spectators, and volunteers a palpability to meet and know the dogs and mushers.

Access to water was quite different during the early races. Many of the villages did not have running water; therefore, considerable amounts of additional time and energy were required to attain enough water to maintain the dogs. We used our axes to break the ice in the rivers or lakes in order to get water. After a couple years of racing, the villagers would cut holes in the ice to expedite our time at the checkpoint. The villagers who allowed us to stay in their homes heated pots of water on their stoves; warm water upon arrival decreased our checkpoint stays by 45-60 minutes. The checkpoints today have barrels of water boiling or taps that are accessible for the mushers to get warm water thereby increasing their efficiency at the checkpoint considerably.

When camping on the trail, we used our axes to chop wood to build fires and melt snow from the trail for our water source. We packed Coleman® stoves on our sleds for cooking in case we did not reach a village before dark or did not have a campfire. Tang® was the flavoring of choice to disguise the smoky flavor of the water. A checker from Finger Lake thought of the idea to use Heet®, which is methanol, to burn in a cooker with a stainless-steel pot lodged atop in order to melt snow. A cooker and pot are now mandatory gear carried in the sled bag so there is always the availability to melt snow and have food and water for the dogs. Transporting food for the dogs between checkpoints is mandatory, also.

The early races organized the mushers to stay with families in their homes when we reached the villages. It was Alaskan hospitality at its finest. There are families that I had the privilege to watch their kids grow-up from year to year while running the race because I stayed with them on an annual visit. Corralling rules were instituted during the mid-80s which now designate all racers to stay at the checkpoint.

Today's Iditarod requires not only mandatory equipment and supplies be carried on the sled; it also requires certain specifications of the gear. The sleeping bag I used in the 70s was an Air Force GI mummy bag which was goose down with an outer shell. It weighed 6-7 pounds and was bulky consuming a considerable portion of my sled bag which, at that time, was a set of military-issued duffle bags. Textile specialization has produced better, higher quality sleeping bags, gloves, parkas, dog coats, etc. that are lighter weight and compressible. Layering of clothing to maximize the efficiency of the material is empirical. Temperatures can range from 40 above to 40 below zero degrees °F within a couple hundred miles or less. Wind intensifies the cold. Strategies to layer polypropylene, fleece, wool, down, laminate fabrics for wind blockage, etc. are important to experiment and perfect long-before race time. I, personally, prefer a polar fleece shirt and pant ensemble as a base layer that a friend of mine sewed for me years ago. Whatever fabrics are used, the key is to stay dry and keep your core warm.

The canine medical team has grown in accordance with the size of the race. Veterinarians, vet-technicians, and care-providing, non-medical people from all over the world volunteer their time and talent to assist mushers and officials to care for the dogs racing in this event--as well as, many of the other dog-sled races around the world. Each checkpoint is staffed with a team of these individuals available to assist the musher for evaluation and care of their dogs. If the musher chooses to "drop" the dog, meaning the dog will no longer race, the team assumes care of the dog until the dog can be safely flown to Anchorage and picked-up by the musher's handler for continued care. Every musher must have a designated handler for this purpose prior to the start of the race.

As an effort to provide optimum care of the dogs, before participating it is mandatory that every dog receives a thorough health physical by a veterinarian, an EKG, as well as laboratory chemistry panels and complete blood counts. All of this data is tracked, evaluated, and correlated with any issues that may, or may not, arise. Studies are underway each year to test and evaluate issues affecting our dogs. In addition to the comprehensive assessment and examination, all of the dogs participating are required to be treated for Echinoccocus multilocularis two weeks prior to racing to avoid transmission of this parasite to other dog teams and/or the villages and wildlife in the interior of Alaska.

Drug testing for any enhancing, steroidal, anti-inflammatory agents is also conducted; the use of these agents is strictly prohibited in sled dog racing. Our dogs perform on their natural ability coupled with proper conditioning and training. Conditioning focuses on their physical well-being; training focuses on their mental and emotional welfare. Mushers must be proactive throughout the year to maintain healthy aspects regarding both of these concepts. Socialization is a huge factor for today's racing dog. At the race start, there are spectators and handlers coming at these dogs from all directions with music and loud-speakers blaring in the background. When the dogs reach a checkpoint, they must be prepared to bed-down and rest in straw with, literally at times, dozens of dog teams around them with teams coming and going. Our dogs need to be readied for that type of interaction to eliminate undo stress. For example, it is not uncommon for mushers to put 'dummies' on their training trails or integrating different sounds in the kennel to prepare the dogs. The dogs of 30 and 40 years ago were more reserved and skittish by-in-large, but were notably trust-worthy and resilient to perform when these concepts were not as universally instituted. Again, many of the early-years' dogs represented kennels from remote places with minimal human interaction comparably.

The International Sled Dog Veterinary Medical Association has been formulated with veterinarians world-wide who strive to improve care, safety, and welfare of sled dogs. Study and evaluation of data is not exclusive from ultra-distance races, Alaska, or the U.S. Veterinarians from Europe and Scandinavia present data and institute research projects from their home countries. Exchange and transference of information from these practices has built a database of evidence-based information to enhance protocol establishment, research, and medical management. The medical input from this research has promulgated into standards of care, nutritional guidelines, genetic study, and integration of complimentary disciplines. The cascade effect is this information is not only available to veterinarians assisting working dog populations, but a resource for the veterinarian providing care for your family pet.

The volunteers involved with Iditarod are never thanked enough and have escalated this race to its magnitude. Volunteer efforts start months in advance in preparation for the race. Volunteers are: handlers at the race start working, pilots flying their planes, snowmobilers on the trail, villagers at each checkpoint, the veterinary team, inmates at the Correctional Facility near Anchorage to care for 'dropped' dogs until the designated handlers are available, and many more. Volunteers staff all checkpoints and provide food, water, and a warm place out of the cold 24 hours a day until all racers have passed the checkpoint. For some of the checkpoints that require mandatory rest, there are days volunteers generously serve to support the race, dogs, mushers, and officials.

Want to run Iditarod? Start saving money now! I read years ago, circa 2010, the average cost of running Iditarod was $59,000. Some established kennels with veteran mushers are able to race for far less money; however, rookies and other mushers with different circumstances require a more substantial sum. Costs quickly amass due to a variety of reasons:

Dogs—This is the best part of the investment; it is not just any dog that is capable of running today's Iditarod. A musher can start the race with 14 dogs, but it usually requires a pool of 20-24 dogs during the season to fill the roster barring injury and other training issues. For the kennels that have breeding programs, add puppies and retired dogs to the numbers that do not participate in the race.

Food—Olympic athletes build and fuel their bodies with high quality, nutrient-dense foods and we feed our athletes correspondingly. The average cost to feed a dog is approximately $2 per day, per dog depending on time of year and caloric needs; this is 365 days a year — racing or not.

Medical care — Vaccines, liniments, supplements, incidentals, diagnostics are some of the obvious costs. Much like people, issues arise in dog teams and kennels; expenses amass quickly to provide care for all dogs in the kennel, not just the ones running or racing.

Entry fee — Current entry fee is $3,000 to $4,000 depending if one's entry fee is submitted before stated deadlines in the race rules.

Sleds and Equipment — Cost for a permissible sled that upholds the requirements of the race rules is approximately $3,000. Harnesses cost an average of $20 to $50 — per harness. Gang-line sections with a reinforced cable-fill for added strength and is chew-resistant costs approximately $25 to $38 per 2-dog section. Booties cost approximately $2 to $3 per bootie. Collars, bowls, cookers, etc.

Freight and Logistics — Several days in advance of the race, the musher must assemble drop bags full of food, gear and various necessities to be available at the checkpoints when the musher and their team arrive at the checkpoint. The bags are loaded on pallets and flown to the checkpoints. If the musher lives in the lower 48, the drop bags need to be freighted to Anchorage weeks in advance so there is freight to Alaska then freight within Alaska. Lastly, when the musher arrives in Nome at the end of the race, the dogs, musher, and usually a handler have to return safely to Anchorage by plane. The dogs have to be secured in airline kennels and if the musher does not have that coordinated in advance, the kennels require purchase.

Travel — Mushers must have a vehicle or trailer for transport. This vehicle requires 4x4 capability and heavy-duty enough to transport at least 14 dogs (800-1000 pounds) plus food, gear, meat, sleds, etc. Rarely do these types of vehicles average greater than 20 miles per gallon, and usually, far less. If a musher is traveling from the lower 48, the expense of travel is several thousand dollars just to get the musher and team to Alaska. The Alcan Highway is the main passage through Canada to

Alaska. As a side note, the Alcan Highway has significantly improved over the years. Many of the years I traveled the Alcan, several sections of that highway had not yet been paved.

Race qualifications—A rookie who desires to run Iditarod must demonstrate and achieve various qualifications:

"Standards for ITC (Iditarod Trail Committee) Approved Qualifying Races

All qualification Races will be approved by the ITC based on the following criteria:

1. A race wishing to be approved as a qualifier must have at least a one year track record, or the race organizations wanting Iditarod approval for their race to be a qualifier must have at least a one year successful track record, the request for qualification status be presented to the ITC Rules Committee by sign-up day, and that an annual review of all qualifiers take place.

2. Qualifying Races will have a minimum distance of a certified 150 miles.

3. Qualifying Races will have at least one licensed veterinarian on race courses until the last team is off the trail.

4. Qualifying Races...will submit for each qualifying musher a completed "Musher assessment form" (Report Card) provided by the ITC to the participating Qualifying Races."[4]

Want to finish Iditarod? Iditarod finishers number fewer than those who have summited Mount Everest. I recommend a person who desires to finish the race seek an experienced musher with an established kennel where an apprenticeship is an option. Training for the musher starts from the ground up which means with a rake and a scoop shovel. A great deal of knowledge is gained when observing and working in a kennel to learn dogs—conformation, mindfulness, desire of the dogs coupled with kennel management of discipline, conditioning, training and care. After appropriate training, run as many races as time and resources allow. This will take a couple of years to really know the dogs. After qualifying races have been completed, devise a race strategy early in the season to implement training/conditioning accordingly. For example, if one plans to race their team of dogs on a schedule alternating 6 hours running then 6 hours resting, it is important to institute the same schedule during training. Leasing a team/dogs is also an option, but I believe the same concepts noted above apply.

It is noteworthy to mention the winning team's average payout for years 2012-2017 was approximately $61,000 in cash and a new Dodge truck-- that is the winning team. Teams that do not win, receive substantially less cash and no truck. Obviously, mushers do not do this for the money.

---

[4] © Iditarod Trail Committee (October 2016). Iditarod Trail International Sled Dog Race Official Rules 2017. Retrieved from Iditarod.com/race/rules/Rule 1.

Indeed, the Iditarod has comprehensively evolved over 40+ years and weathered many storms. With the exceptional individuals now involved on Iditarod's many levels, I envision continued progress. Associated veterinarians and mushers alike are now confident our dogs are the toughest, most resilient athletes in the world. One of the best measurements of aerobic potential and overall cardiovascular fitness is called maximal oxygen uptake (VO2 max.) With great pride, I have learned that some of our sled dogs have measurements almost 2 ½ times that of the greatest recorded Olympic athletes and Tour de France winning cyclists. Sled dogs have significantly out-performed thoroughbred horses' measurements also. After speaking with the sports-medicine veterinarians currently active in these studies, we feel there are modalities and practices that will fortify continued progress in the sled-dog world. Our greatest focus is what we can do to improve the welfare and safety of our canine athletes while unleashing their potential. With education, support, and coordination for all persons involved, we will preserve the grand specimen of the working sled dog and their treasured bloodlines.

Dr. Terry Adkins/Jean Wise

Tales of the Trail

Tale 1: Joe Redington, Sr.

The 'rule of thumb' is the average sled dog is able to pull approximately 3 to 5 times his or her weight. Obviously, the more dogs hooked together and pulling exponentially increases the power generated. I once heard Joe May say it best in reference to the size of a dog team, "Every dog over 9 increases your terror factor by 1."

In the 70s, there was no rule mandating a limit on the number of dogs allowed to start the race. Joe Redington, Sr. seized the opportunity to start the Iditarod race with 23 dogs hooked up and his son riding with him, all the while dragging a tractor tire in an attempt to control the dogs. Several miles down the trail, Joe released the tractor tire trailer and assumed the team by himself.

That night between Knik and Skwentna, I came upon a big blob moving down the trail. I could see something dragging behind a sled. There was a mass of dogs and something dragging in front of the sled. I yelled, "Joe, is that you?" The only reply was an imploring "help."

I stopped my team, set my snow-hooks and ran to the moving blob. The caboose of the blob was a dead tree stump tied to the sled and dog team. I navigated past the stump to the sled and set the snow-hook as firmly as possible to stop the team. A quick inspection revealed the object dragging in the middle of the dog team was Joe tangled with a couple of dogs. In front of and behind Joe, dogs were pulling, some of which were tangled yet still pulling. Lines were everywhere—neck-lines, tug-lines, gang-lines, lines under harnesses, lines under legs… and a bunch of eager dogs pulling. It would have been a mess in the daylight, but was utter chaos in the dark of night. I helped Joe unveil himself from the disarray of dogs and lines then further assisted to straighten the team into a functional assembly. Joe explained one of his dogs became tangled in a line, so he stopped the team and used his snub line to tie to a dead tree stump to hold the team. While he was untangling, the other 20+ dogs lurched and ripped the stump out of the frozen ground. He was woven into the tangle with a couple of dogs' tug-lines around his legs and arms which made him powerless to stop them, so he was dragged helplessly in the middle of the muddle.

Joe later scratched (he pulled his team from the race) at Elim that year. He had 7 dogs left in his team when he scratched; the other dogs had been 'dropped' at previous checkpoints and returned safely to Anchorage in an airplane. The Iditarod has been an evolution of formulated rules from lessons learned, many times, the hard way. Mishaps like this may or may not have precipitated action. Iditarod subsequently ruled the maximum allowable number of dogs to start the race was 16; years later, the number was further reduced to 14.

Joe Redington, Sr. is revered as the 'Father of the Iditarod' and rightfully so. He was a true visionary. His grasp of success was in part because he lacked the fear to fail. It was never an "if we can" with Joe, it was "how we can." Joe was an exceptionally hardy, adventurous individual with a spirited wit. He raced the Iditarod into his late 70s and remained unceasingly approachable to new and better ideas. In addition, he was able to raise and train sled dogs for the majority of his life while accomplishing many dog-centered feats unrelated to the Iditarod, for example, summiting Mount McKinley with a team of dogs. Joe passed on in 1999, but I hope as the years pass his stated intention for the Iditarod he once shared at a finishers' banquet in Nome does not change:

"Let's keep it a race of men and dogs against the forces of nature. When I need to have a snow-machine allowing me to keep from freezing to death, I'll take up knitting and stay by the fireside. One must know his weakness. Don't run long distance races if you are not prepared for cold weather, or if you panic with the thought of night driving. Don't make a race for the weak; make a race where the weak must get stronger to be able to finish."

Many of us grew stronger thanks to Joe.

Tale 2: The Trail

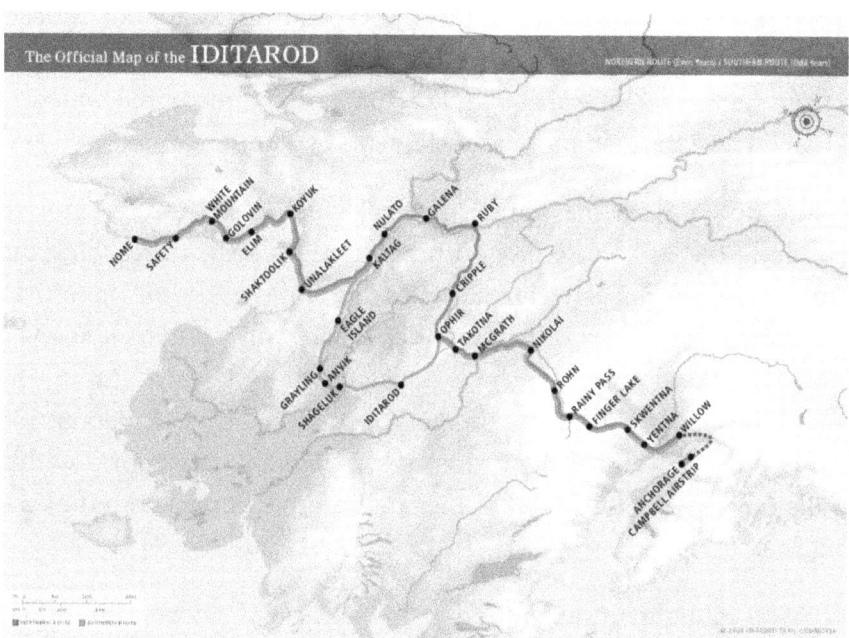

Alaska and the Iditarod Trail possess the best scenery imaginable. Stunning mountains with snow covered valleys laced in streams, creeks, and rivers are a photographer's wonderland. Horizons display brilliant hues of color with the setting sun that silhouette the wild and arctic topography. Night running and camping offer the mystique and awe of the Northern Lights. It truly is a magnificent land. The distance of the Iditarod Trail sled dog race is said to be 1,049 miles, but it varies a little bit from year to year depending on snow and trail conditions. The number of miles traveled is comparable to distances from Atlanta, GA to Boston, MA; from Phoenix, AZ to Portland, OR; or from Minneapolis, MN to New Orleans, LA. Like any of the locations listed, there is varying terrain between places.

---

[5] ©2017 Iditarod Trail Committee, (October 2016). "The Official Map of the Iditarod," Retrieved from www.Iditarod.com/edu/maps/

The first 300 miles of the Iditarod Trail span across the mountainous Alaskan Range; the Happy River, the Dalzell Gorge, and the Burn are included in that stretch of trail. The land is beautiful and wild. Moose, Dall sheep, and caribou are some of the large game of the region I have seen from the sled. The sheep and caribou are interesting to watch as they maneuver the steep mountain slopes.

After the trail passes the Range, it levels for several miles prior to approaching the Yukon River. Within 40 miles prior to reaching the Yukon River, the trail is technical with side-hilling and multiple rises and descents. The Yukon River is indescribably amazing as it spans a mile across in some places. The expanse of the land surrounding the Yukon is humbling. Teams run on the frozen Yukon River for about 150 miles to Kaltag. From Kaltag, teams cross relatively flat country with a few hills on the way to Unalakleet located on the Norton Sound of the Bering Sea.

The coastal climate usually offers a great deal of wind with colder temperatures. The final 200 plus miles is difficult trail to traverse and can be confusing for the dogs. This section of the trail runs on sea ice intermittently, then leaves the coast and scales steep hills and mountainous terrain, which connects to portage trails in and out of checkpoints.

Of any of the sections, the Happy River and Dalzell Gorge generate the most notoriety for inducing thrill coupled with unabashed fear. Those sections are relatively early in the race so the teams usually are quite large, powerful and ready to run. The teams are still running and resting together, meaning the leading teams do not have the distance that separates them from the pack. The dogs sense the energy of other teams and are striving to compete. Therefore, the ride through those sections of trail has been comparable to an amusement park ride at times. I always figured if I made it to the Nikolai checkpoint safely, I could then start to race.

The Happy River has to be a misnomer. The Not-So-Happy River is a far better label for that section of trail. Rookies are usually filled with terror when they reach the spot where suddenly their team disappears over the bank, and a moment later they careen down the series of steep switchbacks to end several hundred feet below on the river. I have been down the Happy River 22 times and every trip I have shouted "Thank you, Lord" upon reaching the bottom. I have seen it with snow so deep it resembled side rails, such as in 1992. In contrast, the years of minimal snow emblazoned my memory when leaves and rocks were exposed and 'road rash' was a threat after tipping the sled. I have gone down on my butt. I rolled down once. I have had to stop when a musher was hung up and had his sled on the opposite side of a tree from his team. My right hand was once broken when I threw the sled into the bank to keep from going over the edge of the last switchback.

The rides through that section of trail were never dull. However, the most exciting trip for me was when a moose was shot by another musher at the crest of the hill. The moose went after a dog team in an attempt to trample the dogs and the musher had to shoot it. The deceased moose remained lying in the trail. When my team and I unknowingly arrived at that section of trail in the dark of night, my dogs ran directly over the moose and started their descent without hesitation. The frozen, deceased beast served as a ramp that launched the sled and me into the air which heightened the terror factor as I saw nothing but the star-filled sky and the nose of my sled. A whipping jerk then hammered the nose of the sled 90° into the ground as I landed. A split second later, the jolt of the attached gang-line combined with the dogs' momentum reeled me and the sled into the most sinuous, steep portion of the trail. Before I knew it, I was helplessly standing on the brake while clenching the driving bow and slamming into the first edge of the switchback. I subsequently bounced to the next berm of the S-curve. The rest of the descent was a blur. I felt like I was the ball in a pin-ball machine as I crashed and banged into trees and snow berms all the way to the bottom.

After Happy River, there is the climb to the Rainy Pass checkpoint. The snow leaving Rainy Pass is usually as hard as concrete due to the windy conditions that are common there. At the end of the pass, the trail turns onto the frozen Dalzell Creek extending about 5 miles as the canyon narrows en route to the mouth of the Dalzell Gorge. The creek remains primarily frozen, but water is seen running underneath the ice yet surfaces intermittently. When the trail meets the opening of the Gorge, there are open holes of water in the ice with fast flowing water visible. At times, there are shelves of ice extending from the bank into the creek. It was on one of these ice shelves my leader, Bony, ventured. I saw the trail meld into the ice shelf and commanded, "haw." Just as I asked, Bony immediately went left and took the team off the shelf and back onto the trail. The team's responsive, quick turn created a whip action that sent the sled and me flailing in the opposite direction on the ice as they turned. The ice sloped downward toward a hole of rapid flowing water. I knew I could not prevent the sled from flying off the shelf and into the water. Not wanting to get any wetter than I had to, I stepped from the runners and unknowingly landed on a patch of black ice. Before I knew it, my feet were higher than my head. I was still holding onto the sled when I went into the swirling hole of the creek. I managed to be totally submerged in the icy waters of the Dalzell. The water was not deep, maybe 18 inches, but lying in 18 inches of water caused me to be just as wet as if I was standing in five feet of water. The water was so cold, it took my breath away. The sled was lodged under the ice shelf where it had fallen. I took my axe and chopped some of the shelf to get dislodged. Between the dogs pulling and me pushing, we made it to dry ground.

I immediately stopped the team and stripped off all my wet gear, poured water out of my bunny boots then put the boots back on because it was very cold to stand on the frozen ground. Luckily it was only about 20 degrees that day and not 20 below zero. Wearing nothing but my beard and bunny boots, I quickly pilfered my sled to find extra gear that was dry. Simultaneously, Ernie Baumgartner and his team rounded the bend and found me stark naked with my rear in the air bending over my sled. Poor Ernie! He did not expect a naked man in the middle of the Alaskan Range nor a moon so early in the day, but the Iditarod trail is full of surprises.

The people, trail, wildlife, and scenery were rarely predictable, yet created an entertaining and challenging allure. Each and every run delivered an array of variables. Running the Iditarod race is a truly unique experience.

Tale 3: After you, Ladies

I have always claimed I am an equal opportunity employer in regard to my dog team. I do not care if the dog is male or female, but rather its ability and desire to do the job. The same sentiment applies for the Iditarod's racers. It would not be fair to contribute the Iditarod's progress without the additions of some truly outstanding women.

The beginning: the idea of re-opening the Iditarod Trail for a sled dog race was envisioned by a historian, Dorothy Page. Dorothy struggled with the idea of losing the sled-dog culture in Alaska when the prominence of snowmobiles and airplanes arose for travel and commerce. Dorothy sought others who were also passionate about the loss of such a rich heritage. She was Iditarod's first secretary and in essence, a visionary for the race. Her tenacity and organizational skills launched mushing to a whole new level. She met repeated resistance but continued with a quiet strength in her actions. What is most notable, to my knowledge, is that Dorothy was never a musher herself. Dorothy is deservingly heralded as 'The Mother of the Iditarod.'

The second year of Iditarod's running, 1974, Mary Shields and Lolly Medley raced making them the first ladies in the Iditarod line-up. The early 70s were a time in history when the women's lib and equal rights movement was a primary battle across our nation. Mary and Lolly catapulted themselves into an arena that was male-dominant, but certainly not gender specific. Frostbite, moose attacks, and blown-out trail do not stipulate the gender of its recipients. Mary and Lolly entered a 'man's world' without request for preferential treatment or exception, but rather with an appetite for challenge and adventure. Their actions sent a powerful message. They were extraordinary people who embraced the sport and the outdoors.

The initial years of the Iditarod were so extreme that it was truly mushing and outdoorsmanship rather than racing. Those ladies broke trail not only for other ladies, but anyone who chooses to race the

Iditarod. Many other ladies slowly, but surely, built up steam to make a difference and 'threw their hat in the ring' of competition in this race. Each had their attributes. Each had their differences.

The most dramatic, in my opinion, was the first time a lady won the Iditarod. The win required a very definitive decision that meant the championship and paved the road for others to trek. Libby Riddles was a slightly-built, blond-haired, blue-eyed lady who lived in Teller, AK. Her 1985 win demonstrated immeasurable courage.

After 700-plus miles and days of racing, several of us had reached the coast. The winds raged with sub-zero conditions and sleet pelted us mercilessly. Several considered continuing on the trail, but the storm conditions were daunting. Libby pulled the hook (the snow hook which anchors the sled and dog team while stopped.) With a team of dogs who trusted her decision, I watched her leave the Shaktoolik checkpoint to go head-to-head with the Arctic coast. I looked to Herbie Nayukpuk, a native of the coast who lived in those conditions and was certainly a pinnacle of silent advice; he rested his team and watched her go. I looked to Rick Swenson, a repeated champion who was no stranger to extreme conditions, adversity, and competition; he also rested his team and watched her go. With many others, we watched Libby pull the hook. I remember it like it was yesterday. She left and everyone else opted to hunker down and avoid the brutality of the coastal storm that ensued. With minimal visibility from the checkpoint, she and her dog team were swallowed by a blizzard and out of sight.

A middle-aged Aleut man with a 'Fu Manchu' mustache was one of the persons watching her leave. He clearly sensed the thoughts that were racing through my mind. With a raspy, yet cautionary voice and clearly spoken words, he leaned within two inches of my face and said, "DOOOON'T GOOOOOO!" I remember the smell of his breath and air hitting my eyes as he held the 'o's. The shear intrusion of my space awakened my psyche. The reality I had been leaning on a coffin that was designated for a local snowmobiler who had been lost and his body had not yet been recovered in a similar storm a couple of weeks earlier ascertained my decision to hunker down with the others.

Libby's guts led her to victory days later. The hours she battled that storm propelled her into a solid lead and she capitalized. We got our asses handed to us...by a girl. It was magnificent! In addition to winning the race, Libby also earned the highly honored Leonard Seppala Award, which is the 'Best Cared-For Team' award--another female first for Iditarod.

Riddles receives Reagan telegram

Nome — Libby Riddles, the first woman to win the Iditarod Trail Sled Dog Race, added to her honors Saturday night when she became the first Iditarod musher, male or female, to receive a telegram from the president of the United States.

President Ronald Reagan's message, one of about 40 telegrams from politicians and other VIP's, was read to a standing-room-only crowd of more than 500 people at the annual Iditarod's Awards Dinner, staged Saturday night at the Nome Armory.

Reagan's telegram said, "Dear Ms. Riddles, Congratulations on your big win! The Iditarod Trail Dog Sled (sic) Race enjoys the attention of fans around the nation. And being the first woman to finish first in its thirteen years, you've caught our attention as well. All the competitors in this grueling 1,135-mile trek from Anchorage to Nome deserve our admiration, but none more than you. You're the winner this year and the honors and accolades you are receiving are well deserved. The state of Alaska and all Americans, salute you on your victory."

Riddles and members of her dog team were honored with several other awards Saturday. Riddles earned the Leonard Seppala Award, voted on by all race veterinarians and given to the musher who exhibits the best care of his or her dogs during the race.

The leaders of Riddles' team, Dugan and Axle, received the Golden Bone Award. Dugan and Sister (who is being re- tired after this year) also earned the Golden Harness Award.

All of the mushers who had arrived in Nome by Saturday night were introduced at the banquet, which was sponsored by Alaska Airlines, Alaska National Bank of the North, Exxon, and Sheffield Enterprises.

Other presentations: Tim Moerlein, the 11th musher overall, won rookie-of-the-year honors; Alan Cheshire and Terry Adkins were co-winners of the Sportsmanship Trophy, awarded to the mushers "who went out of their way to help other mushers, often at the risk of their own disadvantage in the race"; and Raymie Redington won the "Mini 20" award, worth $1,049 and given to the musher with the fastest time from Anchorage to Eagle River, who finishes the race (Susan Butcher actually had the fastest time, but had to scratch).

Also, Lavon Barve won $1,000 and a trophy for being the first musher into Nome; Burt Bomhoff won $2,000 in silver coins for being the first musher to the race's official halfway point, Iditarod; Tim Osmar was presented a trophy for being the first musher to reach Anvik on the Yukon River; Rick Swenson earned a trophy and $500 for having the fastest time from Safety to Nome (22 miles); finishers of the race voted Eagle Island as "Best Checkpoint"; and Howard and Julie Farley of Nome were given the Founders Trophy for their special contributions to the Iditarod.

[6]

At the 2010 Iditarod finish in Nome, Libby and I were standing on Front Street cheering on a Montana gal and her dog team as they claimed the Red Lantern for that year's running—the Red Lantern is last place. Libby proclaimed, "Hard to believe this year's Red Lantern is faster than the year I won it!" Progress. Thank you, Libby, for your contribution.

After Libby, there were years when Susan Butcher reigned champion. Susan was a fierce competitor and claimed four Iditarod championships. She had a characteristic rapport with her dogs. Lead dog, Granite, was a pivotal component of her program. Like many recurrent champions, Susan endured the ridicule of being a champion and its lime-light. Whether you liked or disliked competing against Susan, the fact is Susan was a fantastic musher. Many changes for improved dog-care standards occurred because of Susan's practices. To name just one example, straw

---

[6] Bill Sherwonit, (1985 March 24.) "Riddles receives Reagan Telegram", An Anchorage Times Sports Extra Iditarod '85, E-1.

for the dogs is now mandatory at all checkpoints. She was able to ask more from her dogs because they trusted her to take care of them. Susan loved adventure and outwardly cherished being in the presence of her dogs.

Our sport leaped into public awareness when three of the ten Sportswomen of the Year during the 1980s were mushers: Libby once and Susan twice. The list continues.

DeeDee Jonrowe was one of the longest-running participants of the Iditarod race and had multiple top-ten finishes. DeeDee survived cancer, surgery, and the extended treatment of chemotherapy. The year of her cancer battle, DeeDee completed the Iditarod. The year after that, she got caught in a storm with her team, snowshoed in front of them for miles and finished the race in the top 20. Her tenacity and mettle are masked by a genuine smile and unrelenting kindness.

The support toward the growth of this race has required many non-mushers who affix loose ends and details. Joann Potts volunteered during the mid-70s and made Iditarod a career with a title that mushers agree is the 'glue that holds Iditarod together.' For over 40 years, she has held many positions at Iditarod headquarters; she remains an excellent reference and a trusted friend. She was Iditarod's Honorary Musher in 2016.

Mushing is not just the Iditarod and long-distance treks. Throughout the country and the world, women have earned titles for phenomenal accomplishments in other types of mushing events. Melanie Shirilla has won the International Pedigree® Stage Stop Sled Dog Race in Wyoming four times which was a long-standing record for that race. Those wins have elevated training standards for speed in extended distances. In sprint mushing, Roxy Wright-Champaine was the first woman to win the Open North American Championships in 1989 with subsequent wins in 1992 and 1993. Decades later in 2017, Roxy Wright again won the Open North American Championships—at age 66! In addition, Roxy is the first and only woman to win the Open Fur Rondy, another premiere sprint race in Alaska.

Behind all great mushers is the support of fantastic veterinarians and their medical care, I like to think. The Golden Stethoscope Award has recognized a veterinarian who has been the most helpful on the Iditarod Trail. In 1997, the Iditarod mushers voted female veterinarian, Denny Albers, DVM, to receive this award. A couple years later, Caroline Griffits, DVM was nominated. Both of these individuals have been recipients more than once. Dr. Griffits is also the president of the International Sled Dog Veterinary Medicine Association and the head veterinarian for the International Pedigree® Stage Stop Sled Dog Race in Wyoming.

I like to see new faces and names in mushing. I really wish for new winners. No lady since Susan has won the Iditarod. DeeDee Jonrowe and Aily Zirkle have 'put the run on' several times and captured second place, but it would be fun to see a new face that does not have a beard in the winner's circle. I instructed Jessie Royer from Montana to take Iditarod's title after her teams handily claimed first and second places in Montana's Race to the Sky in 2013 and in 2015. She hasn't done it yet, but my instructions remain the same to her for the future. During the 2017 Iditarod, Jessie accomplished a feat that will never be surpassed; she finished 5th place in the race with a complete, 16-dog team — meaning she did not have to 'drop' a dog due to fatigue or injury during a 1,000-mile race and days of running. Her achievement demonstrated unrivaled skill in animal husbandry, kennel management, team selection, and thorough dog care while participating strikingly competitive. She broke a record I had held for over 40 years which was finishing 'in the money' with a complete team. She just happened to do it better with 16 dogs versus my 12 and a 5th place finish versus my 19th place. I have never regretted giving Jessie her first sled dog over 20 years ago and have been proud as I watched her mushing career prosper. Moreover, it is nothing short of inspirational to see her serene and resolute disposition competing at this sport's highest level with a caliber of dog care that is illuminating a trail for others.

The opportunity to race Iditarod and any other mushing event is available for anyone who chooses to enter. There is no distinction between male and female mushers, it is about the dogs. I have heard men say women have an advantage because women usually weigh less comparably than men and it is less for the dogs to pull. I have heard women say men have an advantage because men are built with greater upper body strength to steer and drive the sled, thus better assist the dogs. I will adhere to the rule applied to my dog team and say, male or female does not matter but rather the ability and desire to do the job.

Tale 4: Physicality

Dogs are a common thread for any variety of people and their cultures. Sled dogs and mushing have a particularly strong fascination because of their oneness with nature and extreme athleticism, not to mention the centuries-old reliance that our ancestors had to these animals. Mushing is a quintessential vision of ruggedness, survival, and determination.

Bob Hope was a comedian I always admired for his passion to serve the United States military and troops. While living in Alaska, Bob Hope visited Elmendorf Air Force Base. My friend and mentor, Lloyd, contacted the managers working with Mr. Hope and offered to give him a dog sled ride. The offer was accepted.

Lloyd asked me to help handle the dogs and be available to assure a smooth experience for such a star. Furthermore, Lloyd needed another musher to provide dog sled rides for the Golddiggers, the all-female singing group that entertained with Bob Hope. My time assisting was not a great sacrifice to state it mildly. The dogs did well and the sled rides went smoothly. The Golddiggers were pleasurable; and during the minimal interaction I had with Mr. Hope, he was a non-pretentious, gracious individual. It will forever impress me how he was able to remember names of the many people he met. He truly seemed to care for people.

While I was living in Idaho, Olivia Newton John was scheduled to perform at Rexburg. I thought she was a sensational country western singer. Prior to her concert, I followed Lloyd's lead and contacted her managers to offer a dog sled ride. She accepted; however, her performance was later cancelled and she did not travel to the area. Days later, I received an autographed picture from her. Soon thereafter, she gained stardom in the pop culture with the hit, "Let's Get Physical."

Both of these stars were eager for the opportunity to ride in a sled behind the dogs. Although it was energizing to be able to meet, or almost meet, the entertainers, they were not really interested in meeting me or Lloyd, but rather, they wanted to meet the dogs.

There was magical allure for me when I began my life with sled dogs. I envisioned beautiful, wintery scenery with a well-behaved, curly-tailed dog team gliding down a gentle, non-technical trail. The 'snap' of reality was hours, nights, and days of training and conditioning the dogs in the mud, ice, wind, and rutted trails. Hours of time were spent preparing food and meat to accommodate the needs of the dogs. Aches and pains from crashing the sled then being dragged by the dog team were a way-of-life. Arm and shoulder strains were impossible to avoid which resulted from hauling five-gallon buckets of food, water, and a combination of the two twice a day, 365 days a year during all seasons, weather conditions, and any sickness. There was also plenty of sheer fatigue from transporting dogs across the country, which includes loading and unloading them into their kennels every four hours on average while they are on the truck.

 The physical efforts needed to take care of these dogs combined with desire of mushing still cannot compare to the strength and internal drive our dogs innately possess. The feedback I have received from most first-time spectators of a race is how enthusiastic the dogs are to go. When we escort each dog to the line (the gang-line attached to the sled,) most of the dogs thrust forward while hopping upright on their hind legs as soon as we take hold of their collars. Once the tug lines are attached to their harnesses, the dogs jump and slam into their harnesses wanting to go. And after they are finally on the trail and running, they do not want to stop and wait.

The trails that are more technical require the musher to truly drive the sled. This takes considerable strength and balance. I have broken multiple bones, teeth, and my ego while on a sled. Some of the shots I have taken to the head probably provide greater insight as to why I still do this. Desire surpasses logic in mushing. As an example, beyond the Dalzell Gorge, the trail reaches the Post River. It was on that river's trail I crashed the sled and whacked myself so hard in the head I saw double for the next couple of days, yet I continued to race. This occurred prior to the 16-dog limit for racing Iditarod, and I had a 20-dog team. For approximately the following 200 miles, I perceived 40 dogs pulling both sleds I was standing on.

I am not complaining. The emphasis is mushing and this life with dogs is not a hobby, but rather a way of life, and a physical one at that. It is all about the dogs. And this undoubtedly requires the individual to be very physically active, just like the dogs, in order to support this lifestyle.

Tale 5: Feeding the Flock

I am frequently asked, "What do you feed all those dogs?" The answer depends on the time of year, the amount of training, and what kind of meat source I have. I have been fortunate to work with a couple different dog food companies to formulate various foods and supplemental products which allowed me to learn a great deal that I integrate into my feeding program. In short, I like to have a high-quality kibble available and several different kinds of meat. For year-round kennel management, I have an 8ft by 24ft walk-in industrial freezer to accommodate the racks of beaver carcasses, salmon, boxes of fat, and the blocks of beef and chicken.

When I was racing the Iditarod, I liked to have several different kinds of meat for each checkpoint available for the dogs such as a buffet of fat, chicken, beef, fish, liver, lamb, and beaver. Beaver has been the all-time favorite meat of my dogs and an appetite stimulate. Trends of my feeding program vary from year to year depending on the most available and economical meat source. Years ago, I got a deal on eggs. The avidin in raw eggs can lead to biotin deficiency in the dogs; so I decided I would need to hard-boil thousands of eggs to safely supplement the dogs' feeding program. Plus, hard-boiled eggs seemed like a logical means for storage. I put a couple of kettles on the stove to boil the eggs. Soon after I started the process, I heard a truck in the driveway that was delivering tons, literally, of commercial dog kibble. I went outside to find the truck was hung-up in a ranch gate at the entrance of my place. We had to dismantle the gate in order to drive the delivery truck onto the premises. After addressing that issue, we immediately unloaded dog food in the feed room. The distraction caused me to completely forget about the eggs that were boiling on the stove.

As soon as I remembered, I dashed to the house and met the smell of eggs while running up the sidewalk. I opened the front door and saw smoke billowing from the kitchen. The whole situation was quite a sight.

There were pieces of cooked egg in the foyer of my house; a clear indication an explosion at some level had occurred. The stove was located over 20 feet from the front door with a staircase, wall, and a 90-degree turn in between. I rushed to the kitchen to find egg pieces hanging from the ceiling like stalactites. Egg debris was splattered all over the walls, windows, and cupboards. Yellow matter was sprayed on the opposite walls of the kitchen over 10 feet away, and there was a watery, egg paste drizzled over the stove and onto the floor. The sulfurous smell was disgustingly intense. Not a single egg of the dozens in the kettle was intact. I spent the rest of the day cleaning up the mess.

When my son got home from school, he immediately questioned, "What is that smell?" I played dumb and replied, "What smell?" The egg experiment required subsequent clean-ups for several days since egg pieces were discovered inside the cupboards, in the dining area, and down the hall. In the end, we had to repaint the kitchen.

Frozen raw chicken has been a staple in my kennel for decades. Cooked chicken bones can splinter which can cause gut perforation in a dog. The raw chicken is fed to the dogs with the feathers, feet, and heads removed. I used to grind the chicken but have resolved the dogs have their own grinders in their mouths. Care must be taken to store and feed the chicken in a timely manner to prohibit bacterial or parasite growth. For daily rations, I usually remove enough chicken from the freezer the day before I intend to feed it because I want to give it to the dogs slightly thawed and chopped into appropriate-sized pieces.

Rod, short for Iditarod, is a large-framed, burly dog who has been a recent member of my kennel. He had a very quiet, stoic demeanor, and was shy to the point of being spooky. Rarely did he demonstrate any emotion. I never knew what he was thinking. His mother is one of the smartest dogs I ever had in my kennel, so I deduced there were 'wheels turning' behind Rod's blank looks. Prior to his first birthday, he had torn an ACL (anterior cruciate ligament) that needed surgical repair. The surgery was performed in the early winter when cold temperatures were problematic for proper healing, so we kept Rod in the house while he recuperated. He was allowed outside for short intervals to go to the bathroom.

My kennel's construction is a barn that houses several dogs with a series of chain-link pens adjacent to it. My property is located several miles from a mountainous area where we are able to train the dogs on snow. I had scheduled a day that we were to train in the mountains. That morning, I took two boxes of chicken out of the freezer to thaw in the basement which would allow easy chopping for that night's feeding. I finished chores then prepared to load dogs on the individual-kenneled, dog truck to transport them to the mountains.

When the dog-truck is backed toward the dog barn, the dogs go wild with excitement. They know a trip to run is on the agenda and when released from their individual kennel runs or tethers, they dash to the truck and try to jump and load by themselves. We had started this process. I had gone from the dog barn to the truck to load a couple of dogs, one of whom was Aug, a muscular, powerful leader of mine. I was lifting him to the kennel on the truck and he suddenly tried to help me by pushing off my chest to propel himself into the kennel. The thrust of his body and back legs cold cocked me directly in the face and knocked me backward, driving me to the ground and slamming the back of my head on the frozen driveway. Aug landed on me and bounced from my chest like it was a trampoline. I just lay there. Aug had no idea what I doing lying around at a time when we were supposed to be loading, so he went and got my partner to help him load. She came around the corner of the truck and found me holding my face and moaning while blood trickled from my nose. After confirming I was okay, she loaded the rest of the dogs until I stopped seeing stars.

We completed some details for the dogs not traveling that day; such as housing Rod, our recuperating dog, in an airline crate in the basement so he would be warm and comfortable while we were gone for part of the day.

We ventured to the mountains and had a beautiful day of running with nice trails and weather. When I returned to the truck from my run, I went to load Aug and turned my head to protect where he had nailed me earlier that day. I do not know how, but he cold cocked me on the opposite side of face and drove me to the ground again! Soon after, my partner returned to the truck with her team of dogs. After watering and giving them snacks, we started the process of loading them onto the truck. As I approached one of the dogs that was still hooked to the gang-line, he darted to the right while I was moving left and the gang-line caught the middle of my lower leg and flipped me into the air and onto my back. I crawled to the truck and watched my partner load the rest of the dogs then we drove home.

Once home, we started the process of unloading the dogs from the truck, and I went to the basement to escort recuperating Rod outside after he had been in the crate for several hours. I opened the door to the basement and could not believe my eyes. Quiet Rod had eaten away a small section of his airline crate, enough to get this head through, and evidently used his teeth to wiggle the box of frozen chicken next to his crate. He proceeded to empty the box through the 6-inch by 3-inch hole he created and evacuated over 30 frozen chickens from the cardboard box into the airline crate with him. He positioned the chickens so he had a foundation on the floor of the crate with a gentle grade where he was reclined and relaxing comfortably…while he blankly stared at me standing agape at the door. The space was so cramped inside the crate with his 70-pound stature and his loot of chickens. Frozen chickens were squashed against the door of the crate with tissue protruding out of it. He had chickens tucked in the corners of the crate 5 high in all 4 corners. I opened the door to the crate and led him outside. He was so proud of himself. For the first time in his life his tail wagged his entire body, his face was alit with a smile from ear to ear, and he was 'wooing' to the other dogs about his great chicken caper.

We fed commercial dog food that night, but Rod was not hungry. After the dog chores were completed, I enjoyed a hot shower, extra-strength Tylenol, ice packs for my face, Kentucky bourbon on the rocks, and a short recess from chopping chicken.

New ideas to nutritionally support the dogs yet make things easier and better to feed are always welcome. I continue to try to provide variety in the dogs' meal plan but have hopefully gotten savvier to the pitfalls that have wreaked havoc like some of the deals in the past.

Tale 6: Sled change

In 1982, one of my very skilled neighbors made a sled I had engineered. He was an excellent blacksmith and used Chrome-Moly to frame and construct the stanchions, then mounted bicycle handlebars for a driving bow. Despite the fact it was metal, it was extremely maneuverable and light weight. I was so proud to take my one-of-a-kind sled to Anchorage and debut my invention.

At the ceremonial start, many offered inquisitive comments, laughs, and inspections. I continued to prepare my sled and dogs for the race. I then saw a familiar, wonderfully revered man walk my way, but he did not greet me. He went to the front of my sled then the side, rubbing his chin and briefly pausing. He then side-stepped to the back then to the other side, all the while he stared at my sled. I finally asked, "Herbie, what are you doing?"

In his usual, resolute voice he replied, "Looking for motor," then illuminated with a smile bigger than himself.

Years later in 1986, I went to Alaska with a bad back and a coordinating cane to walk. I was still using my handlebar sled for racing. Between Knik Flats and Flathorn Lake I encountered a stump protruding from

the right that extended across the trail. I leaned to the left to avoid the stump which elicited a stabbing pain in my back. Immediately, a reactionary thrust to the right crashed me and my sled into the stump. The crash took the first, three feet of my sled runner. The bow of the sled was upturned. With my sled bag supply of duct tape and hose clamps, I attached the plastic runner material to the frame of the sled and tried to continue down the trail. However, every time I put weight on the right runner my sled would flip and my back screamed in pain. I thankfully was able to maneuver the sled to Flathorn Lake.

At the stopover, Bill and Sue Furman and several other people were around the campfire. I was lamenting about my busted sled. Bill quickly interjected that Sue had a brand-new sled in the yard, "You're welcome to it." We referenced the race rules and there was nothing at that time about changing sleds between checkpoints. My team and I left the checkpoint with Sue's new, beautifully constructed wooden sled. The basket was a bit shorter, but it rode like a dream.

I reported my sled change at the next checkpoint and was allowed to continue racing. We were moving well until the tortuous Dalzell Gorge. I advanced into one of the initial descents only to meet a tree limb extending over the trail, which hooked the driving bow of my borrowed sled. In a split second, I saw it change the angle of the bow considerably when I came to a screeching halt and remained attached to the limb. I used my ax and cut the limb and dislodge the sled. We continued to Rohn River where I tried to reinforce the disfigured sled.

After leaving Rohn, the situation worsened when we entered the Burn because there was no snow. The trail was maybe a foot wide laden with sticks intertwined with dirt and ice and protruding tussocks extending 1 to 2 feet high--a terrible trail! The sled's brake twisted into a gnarled pretzel as I used it to slow the team. I was launched over a tussock, and as the sled landed, the top rail crunched in two. The dogs did not care. They kept charging with me flailing behind them while I held tightly to the disintegrating sled. The hardened, frozen tussocks were like slamming into cement blocks and the constant banging to the sled broke the bed slats. Eventually the right runner broke and there was nothing to hook the team in order to keep them stopped for any length of time, so I had to cut the runner off to avoid it tearing off and catching flight. The last thing I needed was an aberrant runner flying through the air which could have impaled me.

We arrived in Nikolai on one runner and a sled that had no usable parts remaining. The plastic brush bow was severely marred but still attached. The left runner also managed to remain in place. Every other part of the sled was broken or torn loose. My nerves were about as shelled as the sled. The bright spot of my trip was that my agonizing back pain paled in comparison to the absolute terror and frustration of maneuvering the team and sled through the previous 100 miles of trail. The dogs, on the other hand, had a pretty fair trip to that point since they had minimal snow to break through or slow them down, and they seemed to have 'drown out' my profanity about 90 miles prior.

Before the race, I had experimented with a Kevlar® sled that I had flown into McGrath. It is/was common practice to have a second sled available at a checkpoint of your choice. My keen sense of the obvious identified Sue's sled would not be leaving Nikolai behind a dog team. I arranged for the Kevlar® sled to be transported by snow machine from McGrath to Nikolai. Unfortunately, after the sled arrived in Nikolai, the condition of the sled revealed no one had ridden the sled to slow it down during the towing process. Evidently the front of the sled continually bumped into the revolving track of the snow machine several times which chipped away little chunks of Kevlar® and created a crack in the bed of the sled. The trail between Nikolai and Ruby was adorned with several bright orange flecks from my Kevlar® sled. The small crack grew into a complete fracture extending through the entire side of the sled during the ride to Rudy. As we covered more miles, the crack widened. Clearly, it was a matter of time before the sled would split in two.

In Ruby, the only replacement sled I could find was an Emmitt Peters 15-foot, training sled. Emmitt was shorter than me so the driving bow of the sled was considerably lower than what I was used to. The brake on the sled was a piece of angle iron which generated minimal resistance, which was an issue since I was still running 15 dogs in my team. Regardless, it was a sled and I appreciated his generosity that allowed me to use it.

From Unalakleet to Shaktoolik, I stood on the angle iron while pulling up as hard as I possibly could on the driving bow, and I still could not slow my team. Blueberry Hill was a blur as I whipped over the trail and prayed not to crash into anything hard.

I reached Nome with 15 dogs, Emmitt Peters' sled, and several I.O.U.s. I paid Sue Furman for her sled, which was totally destroyed. I intended to ship Emmitt's sled back to him in Ruby; however, the cost of shipping the sled from Nome to Ruby was more than Emmitt quoted me to buy the sled. I wrote him a check and sent the sled to Anchorage and had George Ray of Ray's harness shop sell it. Ray said it was easy to sell because it had been used by two Iditarod veterans.

The following year a new rule was enacted that is still in effect today: "… No more than three (3) sleds can be used by a musher during the race after the re-start. No more than two (2) sleds can be shipped beyond the re-start. Should a musher use another musher's sled for any reason that will be considered one (1) of the three (3) allowable sleds. These sleds may be used at the musher's discretion. ..."[7]

I never had sled issues like that in any of the other years that I ran the Iditarod. Materials used in the construction of sleds have improved and many individuals continue to experiment to advance sled design. After all these years, I traded my handle-bar sled for a sled with a seat. The seat, in my opinion, is one of the best sled inventions for ultra-distance and aging mushers.

---

[7] © Iditarod Trail Committee (October 2016). Iditarod Trail International Sled Dog Race Official Rules 2017. Retrieved from Iditarod.com/race/rules/Rule 15.

Tale 7: Lasting friendships

The Iditarod is a race that presents certain situations that often are different each year: terrain, weather, and trail conditions are just a few of these variables. The entrants of the race also yield variety from year to year.

I met a young man when he was a rookie in the early 80s. Our first encounter was an introduction basically, but it was obvious he was an energetic, driven individual. He was very passionate about the dogs and chose an alternative, minimalistic life-style to chase his dream of running the Iditarod. This dream required him to leverage the very last of his resources.

We met for the second time in the Farewell Burn during the race. We had exchanged brief conversation at the checkpoint, but I could not help notice he was riding, like many rookies on a shoe-string budget, an absolutely junky relic of a sled. I surveyed the condition of his sled, calculated the miles and terrain he had yet to cover, then mentioned I had an extra sled in McGrath and he was welcome to it. He graciously declined but was clearly appreciative of the offer. He and the relic made it to Nome to successfully complete his rookie Iditarod run.

The following year's Iditarod that same individual re-entered the race and had a really nice moving dog team. He had paced his team with the front of the pack and was clearly determined to do well. I bid him good luck during one of our checkpoint encounters beyond the Yukon and thought that would be the last I would see him and his team until I reached Nome because his team was moving much faster than mine.

My team and I pulled into Elim a couple of days later and observed a team sitting on the ice a few hundred yards beyond the checkpoint. They left the checkpoint but did not make it far. I asked the checker what happened. The checker explained the musher had been sitting there, on the ice, for about 18 hours. Apparently, his team stalled after a short rest at the checkpoint. Surprisingly, it was that relatively new

Iditarod musher with the really nice moving dog team I had noted earlier in the race. Judging from the position and condition of his team a couple hundred miles prior, my calculations were that he should have left the check point several hours before I arrived. I eventually discovered, he had taken a couple of wrong turns and decimated his front-running standing.

I fed my dogs and rested them on straw for a few hours. As I left the checkpoint, I told the checker I was taking the stalled team with me as I went. Nightfall was looming and it would have been dangerous for them to stay much longer on the ice. I left the checkpoint, went in front of the mutinied dogs, and told the musher to get his dogs up and pack his sled. With encouragement, they followed me and my team. We ran on the ice to the base of what we call Haystack Mountain. By that time, the previously stalled team passed mine; after all, they had rested over 20 hours. The team steadily gained a lead from me and I was losing sight of them. Unexpectedly, the musher stopped his team again, waited for me to catch-up, walked to my sled and said, "Terry, I need to talk. I think my marriage is ending."

We pulled our teams off the trail, fed the dogs, prepared a place for them to rest, and shared some snacks with each other. He articulated the details of his marriage gone awry that weighed heavily on his mind for, approximately, the following four hours. We then readied the dogs and continued to race. Both of us completed the Iditarod that year. He returned to his home and, indeed, his marriage ended. Years later, he remarried and I was the only musher invited to the wedding.

To this day, this man is one of my dearest friends. The Iditarod is not just a race. It is a venue that forages lasting relationships well beyond those with one's dogs.

Tale 8: Eating on the Trail

Traveling across Alaska during the early days of the Iditarod, families hosted us in their homes at each village/checkpoint. It was an education about the various cultures and the resourcefulness of the people who sustained themselves in that isolated and unforgiving region of the world. We were also introduced to various types of food that is very unique to Alaska.

When unable to reach a village before the sun set, we made camp to spend the night under the open sky. Typical protocol involved: feed the dogs, bed the dogs after caring for any need they may have (massage any sore muscles or treat any foot issues,) start a fire, then scrounge the sled bag to find something to feed your face.

Races when I was fortunate to travel with Herbie and Isaac, who were born and raised on Alaska's northern coast above the Arctic Circle, impacted me greatly. Those men had unprecedented abilities of outdoorsmanship; I gleaned whatever wisdom I could from them. Herbie was generous and polite. He once handed me a piece of pilot bread, a non-salty bland cracker, covered with what I thought was butter. Much to my surprise, it was solidified seal oil—it gagged me! Seal oil is a definitely an acquired taste. It warms your body, but it is like drinking lard. From then on, I rushed to make the camp sandwiches of peanut butter and jelly.

After I had raced the Iditarod a couple of times, I was fortunate to have a few sponsors. In 1976 Morrison Knudson, headquartered in Boise, Idaho, was my major sponsor. They had an office in Anchorage and wanted to pack my drop bags in Alaska to avoid shipping expenses from Idaho. They asked me what I wanted in the bags. I was very specific about how much commercial dog food, meat and fat I wanted for my dogs, and in regard for myself I told them, "I do not care as long as it is high in energy, light-weight, and quick to fix."

The race started and upon arriving at the first checkpoint I found the precise amount of provisions I had requested for the dogs, plus 13 Hershey's® chocolate bars for me. The next checkpoint provided the same thing: exact amounts of provisions for the dogs and 13 Hershey's® bars. The following checkpoint…you guessed it. For the remainder of the race, every checkpoint drop bag had the appropriate provisions for the dogs and 13 Hershey's® bars for me. I ate 13 Hershey's® bars while crossing Norton Sound that year.

After completing the race, I returned to Mountain Home, AFB, but I had no energy. I had myself tested at the hospital for various ailments including mononucleosis because of my extreme fatigue. It soon dawned on me I was experiencing sugar withdrawal. It took years before I was able to eat or enjoy another Hershey's® bar.

An all-time favorite checkpoint cuisine was a thick slab of Spam® on a piece of pilot bread. To date, Spam® sandwiches remain a favorite because my friend and veterinarian colleague had provided the sincere offering in Koyuk when my body was craving salt and fat after traveling on the coast. While I enjoyed the sandwich outside the Koyuk checkpoint in the quiet company of my dogs, excerpts of the mayhem that had ensued moments prior to my arrival billowed from the checkpoint just like the remaining smoke.

Three veterinarians, two men and one woman, were traveling ahead of the racers to set-up and prepare the checkpoint to accommodate the needs of the dogs in regard to veterinary care. Set-up at that checkpoint was converting a one-room house into a center for the mushers to eat and sleep. The veterinarians' duties also included food preparation for the arriving mushers. During the set-up, the male veterinarians tried to light the cook stove inside the checkpoint while their female counterpart chose to change her cloths in a corner of the room. She evidently was not as out-of-view as she thought and, rumor had it, was not wearing undergarments. The distraction was overwhelming, and those two accomplished veterinarians accidently set the checkpoint on fire while trying to start the cook stove.   Their innocent, curious glances transformed the scene into a frenzy of fire-fighting mania as all able-bodies combatted flames to preserve the structure of the building. Due to these obvious circumstances, I remain thankful that my friend and veterinarian colleague assumed enough composure to prepare a Spam® sandwich for me--even though it was served cold.

Tale 9: Sleeping on the Trail

"If you want your dreams to come true, don't sleep." — Yiddish proverb

Sleep is a rare commodity while racing the Iditarod. It is beneficial to institute personal practices in training to combat sleep deprivation. Hallucinations and visual disturbances are not uncommon when exceedingly deprived of this precious resource. Obviously, the closer to the race's finish, the more 'rummy in the head' one becomes after logging days of mushing with, literally, just a couple of interrupted hours of sleep daily.

The most recurrent hallucination I have had was trying to duck the horizon as the sun was setting. The hues of fading light with the silhouette of the terrain looked like a wire across the trail I needed to avoid. Within 300 miles of the finish, the coast was a host for sleep deprivation and desperation.

The corralling rule was instituted in the mid '80s. Prior to the corralling rule, the villages' host families welcomed the racers into their homes to stay and sleep. It was a wonderfully kind and generous gesture of hospitality. One of the most memorable stays for me was when I had reached a costal checkpoint in the middle of the night. Arrangements had been made for me to stay at a designated home and when I arrived, the family woke their young son and sent him from his bed to the floor in the living room so I would have a bed. I felt terrible that was the arrangement, but they insisted. The young boy was surprisingly agreeable to be awakened and 'kicked' out of bed. I was exhausted and readily crawled into the empty bed. Instantly my thermal underwear became saturated with urine because the little guy had wet the bed prior to my arrival. I, too, spent the night on the floor, but still appreciated the warmth and hospitality of their home for much needed sleep.

Checkpoints are a luxury for sleep. No matter where the checkpoint is located, mushers tend to establish a routine. Of course, all of us have quirks. I could always rely on Herbie to sleep in front of the door so he knew when somebody was leaving the checkpoint, just like I relied on Jerry Austin to snore--loudly! Jerry was a long-standing musher in Iditarod's foundation. His career spanned over 20 years including the early years. Jerry represented an Alaskan way of life by embracing the outdoors and demonstrating he would do anything for anyone. I always enjoyed racing Jerry and he was a source of endless humor around the campfires. When we camped, we teased Jerry that his dogs could not sleep because of his snoring. Therefore, his winning edge was to get to a checkpoint where his dogs could sleep on straw outside, and he could subject his snoring to all of us inside so we were unable to sleep.

Rest for the dogs is necessary between checkpoints, at times. During a year that had minimal snow, the snowmobilers who were putting in trail for us had broken down before we had reached the Burn. Most usually, if snow conditions are low in the Range, the Burn's trail will be scantily covered, as was the case that particular year. I was traveling within 25 miles from the next checkpoint and I knew the dogs needed rest. I came to an area that had a mound of ice with a snow drift that had blown in. I decided that would be our camp because I could use the snow to melt into water for the dogs. I was traveling ahead of Susan Butcher and when she arrived to that area, she also made camp. I was getting a little 'rummy in the head' because of sleep deprivation. After feeding and watering the dogs, I quickly fell into a relaxed sleep when suddenly I felt my team lurch. I flung from the ground and jumped into the middle of them. A moment later, a bright headlight propped atop Joe Runyan was blinding me. Joe was surprised to find me still in my sleeping bag clenching onto the gang-line in the middle of _his_ dog team! I erroneously had leapt into his team imagining they were mine. My team awoke due to the commotion, but remained curled in balls resting next to the trail. Joe laughed while I and my straggling sleeping bag untangled from the middle of his team. I rested for a couple of hours then we ran to Nikoli where I chose to take my mandatory 24-hour rest and clear my head.

The Alaskan coast can host epic wind storms. While traveling from Koyuk to Elim during the night, I once followed a portage trail that converged onto the trail atop the sea ice where blowing snow and wind made visibility and travel miserable. The trail became increasingly difficult to discern. At Moses Point, I saw a cabin and decided to rest there. I directed the team to the cabin only to find it was padlocked shut. Behind the cabin a 'well' had been created by swirling wind and snow. It was deep enough to protect us from the wind. I piled the 11 dogs I was traveling with into the hole then burrowed with them. Soon after we had nestled in, snow blew over much of the holed entrance. I went to sleep only to awaken with condensation from the dog's breath making our make-shift den extremely humid and wet. My right arm had no feeling and I initially thought I had frozen my hand, but soon realized it was just from lack of circulation since we were a little cramped in there. I massaged the feeling back into my hand after emerging from the hole, assisted the dogs to level ground, fed them, and continued to Elim. Memories of that night and my snow den surface every time I hear the phrase 'three-dog night.' Eleven was a good number to keep warm that cold, windy night on the Bering Sea coast.

Undisputedly, sleep and rest remain a great physical challenge for Iditarod racers. Aspirations and a realistic plan of an Iditarod race is a great, mental challenge for many mushers striving to build a distance kennel. Balance and discipline of the two concepts are paramount to capture the Iditarod dream.

Dr. Terry Adkins/Jean Wise

Tale 10: Lesson in Humility

Running dogs involves the gamut of emotions. Our dogs seem to always have a reserve that is difficult to comprehend. Being part of the Iditarod has been joyful, painful, frustrating, terrorizing, satisfying, educational, and disappointing.

The season of 1992 was littered with disappointing races for me. We did not finish the John Beargrease Race as I expected, despite shattering the race record the prior year. We ran the Montana 500 with a second place finish; although I did not feel my team had the vim of previous teams and I was not passionate about racing the Iditarod. My family provided a great deal of persuasion for me to race; otherwise, I do not think I would have even made the trip.

Lew Freedman wrote an article in an Anchorage newspaper which outlined, it seemed, my internal debate regarding another Iditarod run after a less-than-winning race season. He noted the Beargrease results and the second-place Montana 500 finish then highlighted the monetary winnings provided only enough money for gas to pay for the trip up the Al-Can Highway. Sponsorship was minimal and I had no cash sponsors to appease; so basically, I was running the 1992 Iditarod apathetically. I had privately decided I would scratch early in the race if I felt like it.

I attended Iditarod's pre-race banquet. On my way to the men's room, I was summoned by the 'old guard' of Iditarod headquarters. Starre and Carol, staff members of the Iditarod Trail Committee®, were working the sales tables and motioned for me to speak with them. They insisted I take time to meet someone who had requested to meet me. Starre notified me this person was in the lobby. "Can it wait until I get back from the restroom?" I asked.

"Ok," Starre said, "but don't forget!"

Moments later, I returned to the table per their instruction and they took me to the sunken lobby of the Egan Center. There was an elderly woman who appeared to be in her eighties sitting at a table. She stood with the assistance of two ski poles when Starre introduced us. The lady thanked me for taking the time to meet and continued that she had wanted to meet me for some time since she had followed my race career since Iditarod's beginning. Her face donned a sweet smile and outward contentment. She went on to say she read the article in the paper and was glad I was racing. She had walked from Turnagin Manor to the Egan Center while it was snowing heavily. It was quite a journey in bad weather, but she straightforwardly wanted to tell me, "I think that you are what the Iditarod is all about."

I thanked her and tears welled in my eyes as I helped her to her feet. Starre, Carol, and I watched her leave using her two ski poles to walk as she shuffled past the windows of the Egan Center and disappeared into the swirling snow. Her kind and sincere words pierced my heart. It was what I needed to hear to stop focusing on myself and give tribute where it was deserved.

The following morning, I readied my dogs for the start of the race with a completely different state of mind. I was heading out of the chute to commemorate the 20th running of this great event. I motioned the crowd a big 'thumbs up' as we departed. The dogs performed well and it was a really fun race. We finished in 30th place, which was in the middle of the pack respectably.

The woman's flattering words were as inspiring as her determination. Moreover, it was grounding to address what the Iditarod race is all about which is the dogs—the breeding, training, racing, and care of the dogs. For centuries, working dogs sustained the vitality of Alaska. The Iditarod Race's pioneers founded The Last Great Race® to reinstitute dog power required to access and unite the edges of Alaska. After four decades of racing, the Iditarod Trail Race has remained an annual pilgrimage because of the reliance and vitality of our working dogs.

Dr. Terry Adkins/Jean Wise

Tails of the Trail

Introduction

When God made a dog, He not only created man's best friend, He created an animal that teaches us several lessons. It has been extraordinarily satisfying to traverse the inspiring and humbling Alaskan landscape with many of my best friends.

Eulogy to a Dog

"The best friend a man has in the world may run against him and become his enemy. His son and daughter that he has reared with loving care may prove ungrateful. The money a man has he may lose. It flies away from him, perhaps, when he needs it most. A man's reputation may be sacrificed in a moment of ill-considered action. The one absolutely unselfish friend that a man can have in this selfish world, the one that never deserts him, the one that never proves ungrateful or treacherous, is his dog. A man's dog stands by him in prosperity and poverty, in health and in sickness. He will kiss the hand that has no food to offer; he will lick the wounds and sores that come in encounter with the roughness of the world. When all other friends desert, he remains. If fortune drives the master forth an outcast in the world, friendless and homeless, the faithful dog asks no higher privilege than that of accompanying him, to guard against danger, to fight his enemies; and when the last scene of all comes, and death takes the master in its embrace, and his body is laid away, no matter if all other friends pursue their way, there by the graveside will the noble dog be found, his head between his paws, his eyes sad, but open in watchfulness, faithful and true even in death."[8]

---

[8] Closing argument by Senator Graham Vest Burden v. Hornsby, 50 MO.238

Tail 1: Oscar

With floppy ears, a barrel-shaped chest, splayed feet, and a cow-hocked back-end (where his rear feet pointed outward while his hocks pointed inward,) Oscar was not your typical looking sled dog. He came to me from the Elmendorf Air Force Base dog pound. The men at the veterinary service and I evaluated approximately 140 dogs from the Anchorage and Elmendorf pounds in order to pool 40 dogs that became candidates for an Iditarod team. The evaluation process was pretty basic; we made sure they had a good hair coat and sound feet, then we hooked them up to see if they would pull. We tried every kind of medium-to-large breed dog imaginable. The dogs that did not make the team were placed into homes as family pets. By the time we had selected our team, it seemed most every home on the Elmendorf Air Force Base was proudly sharing their homes with a rescued dog from the pound.

Oscar was a young dog when he entered my life. It took minimal time for me to genuinely adore him. Orson E. Meillot, a master sergeant from my office, named him after me since my middle name is Oscar. Oscar was very gentle, yet an extremely honest working dog. He was clearly intelligent and did not mind leading. Oscar developed stalwart loyalty to me and was an obvious stand-out amongst the conglomeration of dogs we rescued from the pounds.

The 1974 Iditarod was the second, official running of race and the first year that I ran it. The race was still a bit uncharted due to the coordination of details with respect to the distance, which required unbelievable planning to connect Anchorage to Nome.

I was a 'green horn' and arctic trekking was something completely different compared to any other experience in my life. I was raised in Kentucky, and my dad had hunting dogs. My parents and grandparents taught me basics of hunting, fishing, and outdoor life, but the Iditarod adventure was about caring for the dogs in the arctic elements. I had Lloyd Haessler, a sprint musher from Wasilla, as a mentor for training dogs. He and his wife were wonderfully supportive to me with advice and opening their home which allowed me a place to stay and train on their trails; as a side note, Oscar would not run for Lloyd. Oscar ran for me and me only!

My first Iditarod was a phenomenal experience. In those days, the racers ran during the day and camped at night. We did not have required amounts of checkpoint provisions, which are mandatory in today's race. After we had cared for the dogs, we had the opportunity to sit around a campfire with each other. I believe I learned more regarding dog care and outdoor life skills around those campfires than anywhere.

In the whole scheme of things, I had minimal miles of training on the dogs I took to the race. Obviously, the trek took weeks to run so I was quite conservative with the dogs. The dogs were not expected to race at the speed they do today; however, those dogs were tough. Many days we spent breaking trail since it was overgrown and unmaintained. I relied on Oscar as my main leader; he led every step of the race that year. Upon command, he would drag 11 of the dogs to their feet and get them started down the trail.

Oscar ran several Iditarods with me. It was the '77 Iditarod that Oscar proved his unwavering intelligence. We left Unanakleet and traveled on the coastal ice to Shaktoolik. The trail was hard, glare ice and I could not see the scratches of any sled that I thought should have been ahead of me. I was, maybe, a half-mile out on the sea ice and Oscar wanted to cut towards the beach. I corrected him two or three times, but his pace got slower and slower. I scolded him and he continued to steer toward the beach. It was already dark. I saw two lights along the beach, so I relinquished and Oscar took us in that direction. The lights were Ron Aldridge and Lavon Barve who were actually on the trail which ran along the beach. Oscar was correct the entire time we were on the ice.

My team filed in behind Ron and Lavon's teams. We ran for about two or three hours together. In the darkness, the trail was difficult to discern. Ron was in lead but could not find trail. Lavon said his young leader would not go on the ice without a trail. We spotted a light in the distance, probably about five or six miles from us. Ron yelled back to me, "Terry, do you have a dog that you can drive towards that light?"

"Sure do." Oscar led as we traversed blown ice shelves, the graveled beach, and piles of driftwood only to find the light was a man on a snow machine who came from Shaktoolik in search of us. We reached Shaktoolik and spent the night. Ron said he had never followed a dog over such a trail in all his life.

Oscar was a magnificent animal. He did not look like a sled dog, but I would not be writing this book if he had not benefited my life. In essence, I rescued Oscar from the pound and probable euthanization. In turn, he saved my life from the mundane. Oscar retired in Montana and had the 'run of the place' prior to his death. Even though he was unable to run and keep up with the team in his older age, he still liked to work. I trained him to plow my garden. I do not know exactly how old he was when I got him from the pound, although I know he was over the age of 15 when he died the day after Thanksgiving. I buried him in my garden.

Dr. Terry Adkins/Jean Wise

Tail 2: Chinook

My first Iditarod dog team was compiled of dogs from the Elmendorf and Anchorage dog pounds, a couple of dogs that were purchased at very low prices, which included a little female that had a tumor in her eye that I subsequently had to remove the eye, and Chinook. Three days before the Iditarod race, someone gave me Chinook. Chinook was supposed to be a leader and "had run many miles." He was a nice-looking dog weighing over 50 pounds and had the interesting feature of one blue eye and one brown eye. The reality was that I was desperate to find good dogs to complete a 12-dog team roster and was naïve enough to believe anything that other mushers told me.

My first Iditarod began in downtown Anchorage, headed over the Knik River bridges, and then across Knik Flats into Knik which was the first checkpoint. It took all day to get there. I ran a Chuck Raymond Sled which was a racing sled that had a 5-foot long basket. I packed everything but the kitchen-sink on that sled and had room for nothing else. While running on the river ice during the second day of the race, Chinook decided to lie down while the team was running. Not having room in the sled for him to ride, I encouraged him for a couple of hundred feet. I stopped the team and lifted him to his feet, and the next few miles Chinook pulled against his neck-line requiring the other dogs to pull extra. I had no preparations with my sponsor to drop a dog from the race. He was not injured or sore, he just had never been asked to do something like this; so, it was an opportunity to train.

It did not take long to deduce that Chinook was not smart or affectionate. He was very stubborn, but not aggressive. Chinook gradually got into the rhythm of the race. He got plenty of rest each night near the campfire and by the time I arrived in Nome 21 days later with my team of 12 dogs, Chinook was pulling his share of the load. I took those 12 dogs from Anchorage to Nome and finished with an entire team in 19th place, which earned a cash prize. For over 40 years, no one had finished Iditarod with an entire team that placed highly enough to earn money that I am aware; that record was broken in 2017.

The following year Steve Fee, a U.S. Air Force member, ran Chinook as his main leader and finished the Iditarod with him. Steve was very pleased with him. I was thankful Chinook found his niche with Steve. Chinook was a special blue-eyed, brown eyed dog. To this day however, I believe a blue-eyed, brown-eyed dog cannot make up his/her mind about what they would like to be.

Dr. Terry Adkins/Jean Wise

Tail 3: Patsy

As previously noted, I was the one and only veterinarian for the 1973 Iditarod. Herbie Nayokpuk, who later became known as the 'Shishmaref Cannonball,' and Isaac Okleasik were two Eskimo mushers entered in the 1973 Iditarod. After observing those men at several checkpoints, I thought they had some of the best dogs and provided the best care of the dogs in that race. They clearly knew how to survive in the Arctic and embraced the necessity of healthy dogs for that lifestyle. There was a great deal of information to gain while simply observing them pack and unpack a sled.

At one of the checkpoints, I diagnosed a dog on Herbie's team with an inguinal hernia. She was a completely white female and a very hard worker; her name was Patsy. I told Herbie that there was a possibility the hernia could strangulate her intestines and cause serious problems, potentially even death. I pulled the dog from Herbie's team. Herbie said, "You doctor, you fix."

I had Patsy flown to Anchorage where my assistant, Dr. John Gamby, performed hernia repair surgery on Patsy. Prior to her return flight to Nome in order to reunite her with Herbie, I was very interested in the dog and I asked Herbie if he wanted to sell me the dog to avoid unnecessary flights.

"No. Patsy house dog, not for sale."

A year later, in 1974, I raced a team in the Iditarod. I finished the race and deemed that would be my one and only time across the Iditarod Trail. I was sitting in a bar in Nome when a bush pilot, Larry Thompson, entered and said he was flying to Shishmaref. Larry asked if anyone wanted to go with him. I said, "That's where Herbie lives." He confirmed my statement and invited me to join him to visit Herbie. We jumped in his plane and flew to Shishmaref, a village on an island north of the Arctic Circle in Alaska.

Herbie's home at the time was a one-room cabin that had a cook stove in one corner and a 50-gallon water drum for melting snow in the other corner. There were blankets partitioning the cots where his daughters slept. The homes in remote Alaska were stark in relation to most standards, but the hospitality was warm and grand. I was not aware the culture encourages gifting something to the friend who enters their home. Soon after I entered Nayokpuk's home, Herbie presented a walrus skull with two long tusks as an offering to me. In those days, that ivory was valued at over $1000 and it would be 3 or 4 times that today. Shocked by the immense generosity, I said "Herbie, you can scrimshaw all that and make some money on it. I don't need that walrus skull!" After I thoughtlessly uttered the words, I realized I had offended Herbie by not accepting his exceedingly generous offer. Without hesitation he turned to one of his daughters and directed, "He like Patsy. Get Patsy." The daughter returned with the white dog I had diagnosed, arranged surgical repair to be completed, and offered to buy the previous year. Not wanting to offend him a second time, I took Patsy and returned to Anchorage where I was living at the time.

I do not think Patsy was a house dog because she shed her coat four times when I got her to my home in Anchorage. I surmise she had lived on the sea ice in the most austere conditions and was an example of survival-of-the-fittest. Herbie was good to his dogs; thus, they were good working dogs; there seemed to be a mutual reliance for survival. Herbie hunted every species of the arctic; the dogs were with him and provided travel in the rugged terrain. His dogs adapted to the elements, just like Herbie. I bred Patsy to an Eskimo dog I bought from Stanley Barney, named Lingo. To this day, my kennel is beaming with white dogs descending from Patsy.

Herbie was charismatic and had a highly contagious smile and laugh. Herbie was noted for his generosity and benevolence, yet was as tough as anybody ever made. With indescribable humility, Herbie changed my life the day he graciously gifted Patsy to me.

[9]

---

[9] Images are signed mail caches. These caches were carried on the sled from Anchorage to Nome in 1974.

Tail 4: April

April was a daughter of Patsy with three other littermates: Herbie, Isaac, and Blaze. As a puppy, April was a little, white bundle of joy with the vigor and newness of April, hence the name. As she grew, she became a sometimes crabby and feisty dog that had a vindictive, jealous streak in relation to me and other dogs. Her bloodline graced her with terrific efficiency; she did not readily eat but growled at any other dog that looked at her food. Despite any of these shortcomings, she had an unprecedented allegiance to me and did anything I asked. She embraced her job eagerly and was a fantastic gee-haw leader, trail leader, and race leader.

April was with me in 10 Iditarod races and led several of them. Her career spanned during the early Iditarods when trail conditions were more extreme and required a tough-minded dog to endure all the elements while traversing remote Alaska. She was brilliantly intelligent, had a sweet soul with contrasting grit, smiled beautifully, and had an inherent ability to lead. April was my pride and joy.

April became a leader early in her career on the coast going to Nome. I had travelled the entire Yukon River with Rich Burnham. At the time, Oscar, was my main leader. Rich and I were between Unanakleet and Shaktoolik when an Arctic fox ran 200 yards in front of my team. April was in swing, the position of dogs directly behind the leaders, and saw the fox. She immediately charged past Oscar, knocked him to his butt, and took the entire team down the trail trying to get to the fox. I set my hook, ran to the front of my team, changed Oscar to swing position and put April in single lead. She charged when we went past the place where the Arctic fox had crossed the trail. We then went into an area that had a lot of ptarmigan flittering amongst the trail. As the ptarmigan burst from the snow, April jumped in the air and run that much faster. That remarkable athlete was capable of jumping and bounding along the trail after 700 miles of racing.

As I noted earlier, I traveled several days with Rich Burnham. After I put April in lead, we traveled a great deal faster and she got us to Nome 24 hours before Rich arrived; this is an example of a trait is needed for a good leader — to energize the team which usually increases the speed.

April was the type of leader that enjoyed to race, yet had patience to allow me to snowshoe in front of my team in order to break trail. I would then call her, and she would bring the team to me. I do not think she ever stepped on the tail of my snowshoe nor tripped me for the miles we traveled in that fashion. She would hold a team behind her until I would call. She is the one-and-only dog I ever had that displayed that type of leadership.

---

[10] ©Jeff Schultz photo. (Early 1980s). April leading Terry Adkins Iditarod Team out of the starting chute.

Capable to lead teams into the back-country of Wyoming for elk hunting excursions, April once returned a 15-dog team to me after their lurching straightened the eye-bolt that secured my snub line to the truck. The team burst from the truck and proceeded to run up the hill without me and the doctor that was hunting with me. I called for them. With April in lead, she swung the team completely around to return to me. This is very unusual and remarkable quality for a leader since we train our leaders to keep ahead of the team so they are not over run by them.

April had protective qualities which are unusual for a sled dog. I once tied her to the back of my sled while at a checkpoint because she was in heat. During the night a group of individuals pilfered several of the sleds that were parked at that checkpoint. My sled with April sleeping on top of it was untouched.

April whelped one litter of pups. I name my litters with a theme and the litter's theme was beer—Oly, Blatz, Lite, Schlitz, and Bud. Oly, another main leader and a primary breeding stud, was an amazing dog which I will discuss later. Lite was a little female. April and Lite hated each other. Those two females had immense jealousy of each other, and I had to run them completely apart in a team. I placed April in lead and Lite in the wheel position--the position directly in front of the sled. Those inner-kennel rivals were pivotal dogs in my team for many years.

At age 14, April was afflicted with a mammary tumor that I excised; however, another tumor returned when she was 16-years old which subsequently caused her demise. As painful symptoms manifested, I decided I had to euthanize her to prohibit any suffering. At the same time unfortunately, Lite who was 12-years-old, had developed a rapidly growing vaginal tumor. I euthanized both dogs on the same day--crying all the while. I will probably pay for this decision at some point in my eternity, but I buried the two of them in the same grave in my backyard. Their jealousy and animosity died that day and they were laid to rest.

Decades later, playful, willful, and feisty tendencies with loving, contented faces surface in many of April's descendants. It thrills me to see her qualities and I relish the memories of a one-in-a-million dog.

Tail 5: Herbie

Herbie, named after Herbie Nayukpuk, was a brother to April. His burly frame with a symmetrical dark brown and white coat made him an absolutely beautiful husky. He was hardy and tough. I do not remember him ever being injured and he ran nearly as many Iditarods as April.

Dogs are amazing. Over the thousands of miles I have run with dogs, their endurance and stamina is prodigious. Equally impressive is the memory and thought processes of dogs. Herbie taught me early in my mushing career the capacity of their memory.

Herbie was leading on the stretch of trail into the McGrath checkpoint, approximately 300 miles into the race. There are a number of portage trails into McGrath and we had taken one that had knocked off a couple of miles for us. We finished in Nome that year approximately 700 miles later.

The following year was a heavy snow year and Herbie was leading the team from Nikoli to McGrath. As we neared McGrath, Herbie suddenly jumped off trail into about three feet of snow. I called him to return to the trail and he looked back at me in confusion. I then realized he was trying to take me on the portage trail he had taken the prior year; however, it was not open due to the increase in snow. Herbie did not care. He gave a look as if to say, "We went there last year. We should go there this year." And he was willing to bust through three feet of unbroken trail to do it while pulling a team behind him.

I know that many of my dogs were able to remember trails better than I did. When running a dog team for extended distances, I rest the dogs for short intervals every couple of hours and schedule times for them to stop and snack. It has been the norm, more than the exception, for dog teams to stop along the trail at a spot where we stopped to snack during the previous trip.

Herbie was indeed a beautiful dog with a terrific mind, in addition to being wonderfully calm and steady. Retrospectively, Herbie was pivotal instruction for me to watch and trust what the dogs try to say.

Dr. Terry Adkins/Jean Wise

Tail 6: Bony

11

Bony fit her name. She was one of the lankiest, boniest dogs I have ever seen. Her head was smaller than her neck, which deemed her capable of slipping any collar. She was brownish in color with floppy ears. Bony was a sweet and lovable dog. When she ran within the team, she maintained a tight tug line; however, when she led, she did not work as hard at pulling and was a beautiful 'steering wheel.'

Unrecognizable from her stature, Bony had a voracious appetite. While staying at Lloyd Hessler's kennel prior to the Iditarod one year, April delayed eating like she usually did. And true to form, Bony slipped her collar and took advantage of the situation devouring April's food. April lit into Bony and a fight ensued. April was cut on her left shoulder and

---

[11] Gregg McConnell photo. (1983, Feb 8). Dr. Terry Adkins holds "the real champion", Bony, after a 1st place finish in the Governor's Cup sled dog race. Ravalli Republic, p1.

I had to stitch the wound, but for the following days, the dogs acted as if nothing happened.

The Iditarod race has a ceremonial start in downtown Anchorage followed by the official restart the next day. During this particular year, the restart was at Settler's Bay. The race attracts hundreds of fans and spectators that line the first couple of miles of the trail. When my team and I arrived at the starting chute, I had my trusty, lead combo of Bony and April since they were hard working, reliable dogs that had run, literally, thousands of miles together. I never imagined there was a grudge between the two of them after the dog food stealing incident. To my surprise, Bony and April erupted into an epic fight. I immediately set my snow hooks and ran to the fighting dogs. Yet within seconds, significant damage resulted. April bit Bony several times in the legs. Bony's tongue was torn either from April's gnashing, or possibly biting her own tongue during the commotion. Either way, blood covered white-coated April. The snow in the starting chute was blood-tainted. I was busy with the two dogs, unable to hear the gasps from the crowd due to the unfortunate scene.

I quickly took Bony out of lead and put her in the team. We started the race, but within miles, Bony's legs started to swell. I loaded her in the sled and hauled her for the next couple hundred miles. I returned her to the team a couple of miles before the McGrath checkpoint. Bony's legs swelled again when she began to run, so I officially 'dropped' her in McGrath where the veterinarian team could provide thorough care prior to her return flight to Anchorage.

Years prior to the 'Starting Chute Massacre,' Bony earned the esteemed honor as the best coastal leader I have ever run. The first year Bony ran on my team during the Iditarod, we reached the coast without event. I rested my team in Shaktoolik. We left there well into the night. Within a few miles after traveling on the sea ice, I discovered the tide had come in and all the trail markers, which were spruce bows at the time, had been taken with the overflow. A mild ground blizzard had also developed, which made the trail completely undetectable. The sun had set hours prior so it was completely dark. The trail was washed out and refrozen, turning it into essentially glare ice. A fog descended upon us completely prohibiting visibility. My headlight shining into the fog made things worse, so I turned it off. It was eerie. I could see absolutely nothing including my dogs while moving on the sled. I could hear nothing except the dogs breathing and the sea ice cracking below us. I debated turning the team around and returning to Shaktoolik; however, they had just rested and were ready to run. Furthermore, if I had attempted to turn them around without completing 180-degrees, I could direct them off the ice and into the open waters of Norton Sound.

Bony had previously run that section of the Iditarod trail at least twice before. I stopped my team and put Bony in lead. She acted like she knew where she was going, so I spoke minimally to her as we zipped across Norton Sound in approximately six hours. I must admit it was unnerving, actually undeniably terrifying. The darkness and fog made me feel like I was in a tunnel. There were absolutely no landmarks or change in trail for hours. I did not see a trail marker until we got within 5 miles of Koyuk. The lights of Koyuk were the most beautiful things I had ever seen in those early, dark hours of that morning.

Reflecting that time of my life, I know of no other being who earned that kind of trust...except maybe April. Bony could have taken me and the other dogs into the waters of Norton Sound, or she could have cut to the shore where we would have been lost. I knew the dog remembered the trail. Silent uneasiness plagued me and I am convinced the dog knew it. Bony never hesitated; she maintained a brisk pace. In fact, in the twenty-plus years I have raced in the Iditarod, the night of 'Bony's run' was the fastest passage on Norton Sound any of my teams have ever made.

Bony, the best coastal leader I ever had.

Tail 7: Oly

Oly was the son of April and a dog named, Boy. Boy was a tough Eskimo dog who was the one and only dog I had ever seen fall asleep while running in harness. He would lean away from the gang-line, step off-trail awakening himself, and then return to pulling with a tight tug-line. Boy had beautiful conformation and a pleasant, mellow personality. The breeding with April was paramount to produce the patriarch of my kennel.

Oly was my main leader for several years and completed ten Iditarod races. Actually, he ran eleven, but I scratched one year at Galena — meaning I withdrew the team from the race because I was afflicted by vestibular neuritis.

Oly was a blocky, 68-pound, white male with marble eyes. His desire to fight was a close second behind his desire to run, and his yearning to breed superseded both of those pastimes. He was stubborn, cantankerous, aggressive, aloof, and limitlessly stoic. Yet I loved him dearly and completely.

In Oly's first Iditarod, he quit pulling and actually neck-lined before approaching McGrath--meaning he pulled against the line hooked to his collar creating more work for the dogs ahead of him. I attempted to load him into the sled to rest and ride, but he refused to stay. He and I engaged in a wrestling match during several attempts to make him remain in the sled bag. He won and my patience lost. I threw him in the snow next to the trail and muttered, "If you won't work and won't ride, I guess you'll have to stay here!" I got on the sled, called up the team, and proceeded down the trail. Oly looked around in the darkness as if to say, "He is really leaving me here." He rose from the snow bank and ran to the team. I hooked him to the gang-line and he pulled all the way to Nome. In his entire career, Oly was never loaded on a sled and always pulled more than his share.

During his youth, I often ran Oly in swing with Bony in single lead ahead of him. Invariably, the females always seem to cycle about the time of Iditarod, and Bony was no different. One of the years while running between Kaltag and Unalakleet, Bony led and Oly was behind her in swing overcome with desire. While running, he grabbed Bony's tug-line with his teeth and pulled her toward him. When he released it, it knocked her off balance enough that he was able to grab the tug-line closer to her and repeated the attempt to get ahold of her. On the third attempt and while in motion, he made a flying leap and mated Bony! We were forced to take a 45-minute break while the mating took place. Although I was annoyed at the time, I was blessed with five wonderful pups from that Iditarod love affair.

In the kennel, fighting was a major issue with Oly, and he was always the instigator. His determined soul would fight to the death, and he was merciless to any dog that challenged him. If he got into it with another dog, it took all I had to separate him from the fight. I think it was a bit of sport for him, and he openly cared less that it maddened me. In a perplexing contrast, he did anything I asked while he was wearing a harness and at work.

At age five, Oly decided to use more of his energy to lead. He was phenomenal. His internal fortitude coupled with profound intelligence and unrelenting strength prompted me to evolve in a new direction. He had corporate knowledge of commands after years of running behind great leaders like Bony, April, and Oscar. In his mind, nothing was bigger than himself. There were times when dog teams reached the Yukon River and lead dogs became totally overwhelmed at the absolute vastness and expanse of the river and the country surrounding it. Not Oly. He took our teams to the river and drove. It was obvious he loved river running.

12

The prime of that dog's life were some of the best years of my life. Oly was the trademark of my team and kennel. He ran single lead because he tried to attack anything that was next to him—male or female. He

---

[12] ©Jeff Schultz photo (1986). Oly leading Terry Adkins Iditarod Team.

wanted to be in charge and he did not want anyone next to him. Most often I put his mellow sons, Gladstone and Mike, in swing which created a stable, powerful front end. Thankfully, his aggressive tendencies were not perpetuated in his offspring. Oly was 'all dog.' When I asked him, he did not hesitate to pull all of his teammates off their straw and to their feet after resting at a checkpoint. He simply took care of business for me. Mushing was so enjoyable for me because I had that dog which was dedicated, determined, trustworthy, and did not falter.

Oly was approaching 14-years old when he ran his final, 11th Iditarod-- 1,049 miles. I did not have him lead a great deal of the race simply to avoid undo stress on him. This allowed other replacement leaders to experience the challenges of leading the Iditarod--with an 'ace in the hole' if I needed it. I did have him lead us down the Dalzell Gorge, which he practically walked to deliver us safely through that tortuous section of trail. And, of course, he delivered us to the finish on Front Street in Nome which he so proudly had done many times before.

I retired Oly soon after his final Iditarod because I never wanted him to find out he could be out-done or was unable to keep up in a team. His retirement allowed him to freely roam about my property; yet he primarily sat in a spot directly outside the kennel where he could supervise. He died two days after Christmas at age 17; I buried him at that spot.

Structurally, Oly was an object of perfection and an absolute powerhouse. He and I traveled in excess of 30,000 miles together with combined training and race miles while we covered trails across the lower 48 and Alaska. Throughout that extreme amount of running, he never experienced an injury. Mentally, he was unflappable. Rain, sleet, snow, wind, blown-out trail, nor ice bothered him. He led me through all of it. To this day, Oly's leadership is the standard I measure any dog that may aspire to lead. I have stated multiple times that I currently would not tolerate the boorish, aggressive behavior he exhibited and I can laugh at the enumerable obscene things he did. However, words will never express how deeply I miss him.

Tail 8: Gladstone

Gladstone was a large-framed, solid, red dog with a beautifully mild-mannered and gentle disposition--a total sweetheart. Stoic and apathetic in regard to attention, all he ever wanted was to do his job.

The 1991 season was the first year 9-year-old Gladstone led. He ran primarily at swing, the position directly behind the leader, for the majority of his career with Oly as the primary leader. His dad was such a dominant leader that rarely did other dogs ever lead including Gladstone.

In the early fall of 1990, I started training the team for the John Beargrease Race in Minnesota. The race was a 500-mile run and an Iditarod qualifier. Bill Smith assisted with training and we ran from his kennel in Deer Lodge, Montana. The trail we used was a figure-eight, 12-mile loop with obstacles, including a cattle guard that we crossed with each dog jumping or traversing, an underpass of an active road, a church parking lot, and parallel roadways which can be very difficult for a leader to discern which road to take.

Gladstone made few mistakes in training, but when he did and was corrected, he would subsequently over-correct when the situation arose again to prohibit making the same mistake a second time. He was a wonderfully trainable leader, and obviously, highly intelligent.

On Halloween night, we were scheduled to do a 70-mile run. The temperature that night was bordering too warm to run—the dogs need temperatures about 40 degrees F° or cooler to avoid overheating. I was training 20 dogs at a time and using a Volkswagen chassis for them to pull. I loaded a 5-gallon bucket of water into the chassis so I could rest the dogs intermittently and provide water for them. Despite the warm-weather challenge, Gladstone's tenacity made a fantastic impression on me that night. He led without hesitation several laps of the 12-mile loop when others of his team were ready to return to the kennel. My dog team was not fast, but they were very steady. We traveled, approximately, a 9 mile-per-hour pace and could go indefinitely.

The 1991 Beargrease marathon mandated a continuous 12-hour rest at a checkpoint of individual, musher's choice and a mandatory 4-hour rest at the return Highway 2 checkpoint that was 54 miles from the finish line. My starting position was in the middle of the pack. Most of the mushers were taking their mandatory 12-hour rest at Sawbill prior to the halfway checkpoint at Grand Portage. Evaluating closely, my team looked strong at all the checkpoints solidifying my decision to proceed all the way to the halfway point before taking the mandatory 12-hour rest.

There were reports that there was a vicious team on the trail when I was leaving Sawbill. Vicious dogs that lurch toward other teams are referred to as 'alligators.' My team and I inevitably would pass this team during the next portion of the trail. Prior to leaving the checkpoint, my handler went to the local hardware store and bought an 18-inch piece of plastic pipe; he said, "Take this and put it in your sled bag. Use it on that team of alligators if they come after you!" After all, why would we sacrifice the safety of my dogs because someone chose not to train theirs? I stuck the plastic pipe in my sled bag with the 9 mm pistol I also carried.

Thankfully, the pass with 'Team Alligators' was uneventful. (Just to note how things have changed, it would be illegal in today's racing forum to carry a "whip" or use any type of force on dogs in racing. Not only will any abusive measure disqualify you from the race, it will ban you from the sport.)

We arrived and departed Sky Port, the next checkpoint, in the middle of the night. An hour after leaving Sky Port, we came around a curve and a moose was bedded in the middle of the trail. I reached into my sled bag to get my pistol and came up with 18 inches of plastic pipe as we approached the moose. Gladstone led our team flawlessly past the moose as I stood on the runners behind them with a plastic pipe in my hand. By the time the sled passed the moose with me on it, the moose was upright, startled and annoyed. I hit him on the nose with the plastic to deter any thoughts to charge after us. We were so lucky because dog-team/moose encounters have resulted in dog deaths from moose trampling them on many occasions; mushers have also been stomped by moose attacks.

We arrived at the halfway checkpoint at Grand Portage where I took the 12 hours of rest. On the return leg with a rested team, I purposely stopped my team to bootie them, and allowed Susan Butcher to pass me. This gave me an opportunity to see what her team looked like and how fast they were traveling. I felt that my dogs were moving equally as fast. When we reached the returning Sky Port checkpoint, Susan took a break. I fed my dogs, gave them about an hour of rest while I ate a hamburger, and then we continued to Tofte.

The trail to Tofte is preceded with an approximate 8-mile descent; therefore, an extensive climb is required to return to the North Shore trail when leaving Tofte. After hundreds of miles of racing, there are two ways to get a dog team up a hill: Either forgo rest and continue while the dogs are still in the running mode up the hill, or provide ample rest and allow them to scale the hill partially rejuvenated. At Tofte, I changed booties and gave snacks to my dogs, and then grabbed a tube of Preparation H and treated my hemorrhoids (hours of standing on the runners). These tasks spanned 14 minutes. I had Gladstone spin the team around, choosing the first option. We left the checkpoint and scaled the hill. We were more than halfway up and met Susan traveling to the checkpoint. I could see by the look on her face that she was crestfallen because I was already out of Tofte.

At Beaver Bay, the next checkpoint, the dogs rested until I heard Susan was approaching. I quickly prepared the dogs and led a female leader named Dale Evans, who was in heat, by the male dogs allowing her scent to provide the motivation to get them moving again. We loped out of Beaver Bay and soon met Susan who was just pulling into the checkpoint.

Our next arrival was the Highway 2 checkpoint, which was 54 miles from the finish line. Again, this checkpoint mandated four hours rest. While the dogs rested, I spent the entire time calculating speed combinations. My team was leading Susan's by an hour and five minutes. I figured every strategy imaginable for her to catch us. For example, if she was traveling 8 miles-per-hour and I was traveling 7, how many minutes would it take her to catch us over 54 miles of trail? Anyway, I deduced the only way she could beat me to the finish line was if we stopped. Therefore, the strategy to capture the win was NOT TO STOP!

We left the Highway 2 checkpoint with Gladstone and Dale Evans in lead. After all, the dog-in-heat strategy worked successfully on the previous portion of the trail. Obviously, the dogs were tired so I praised them more frequently than usual to encourage them. I had one little dog that was limping, so I loaded him in the sled. Another dog started holding back as we approached all the road crossings. I also stopped and loaded that dog in the sled. While I was loading him, the other dogs suddenly became very restless and some were barking. When I turned around, I discovered Gladstone and Dale Evans were mated! Clearly, I was no longer on race time and the call of nature inconveniently superseded. And…we were stopped! What was probably a 10- or 15- minute delay felt like an eternity. I strained my neck from the excessive glances I took expecting Susan's headlight to come into view. I cussed a great deal. I paced. I was about ready to throw the intertwined couple in the sled with the other two dogs when they finally separated.

I took Dale Evans out of lead and put Roy Rogers next to Gladstone, then struck towards the finish line. We were traveling in the early hours of the morning and it was dark, of course, but I could see Gladstone was running atypically. He did not limp nor demonstrate pain, just ran unusually.

We crossed the well-lit finish line about 3 a.m., winning the race and setting a course record. ESPN and various other media personnel were there to cover the winning team. I ran to my team to praise them. To my surprise, I quickly discovered why Gladstone's gait was abnormal. The dog's penis had not retracted after the mating incident!

Reporters immediately surrounded us and asked me to put my lead dog upon a bale of straw to conduct an interview. None of these people were aware of the dog's 'situation.' I tried to act as if nothing was wrong and affectionately put my arm around Gladstone while strategically cupping my hand to hide the protracted penis while I conducted the live interview with lights and cameras. Immediately after, I took Gladstone to a darkened area and helped him with the issue. Twenty-eight minutes later, Susan Butcher and her team crossed the finish line in second place with additional racers following throughout day. We had won; however, equally remarkable was the amazing dog that had the fortitude to run the final 10 or 11 miles with such a unique handicap.

The Iditarod was the next event on our schedule. The Iditarod experienced a year of brutal weather with blizzards and excessively windy conditions. We raced for days across Alaska and up the Yukon River with a multitude of weather and trail challenges, only to reach the coast that greeted us with even more frigid and severe conditions.

Between Shaktoolik and Koyuk, the trail crosses the sea ice of Norton Sound. After leaving the Shaktoolik checkpoint, I found we were immersed in a merciless blizzard with temperatures minus 30°

Fahrenheit, falling snow, and severe winds. Visibility was minimal. I had difficulty seeing all of the dogs directly in front me. It was a great relief to note the trail markers sporadically to assure we were still on the trail.

We had traveled a couple of hours on the ice when we came upon a dog team that was lying stalled on the ice. I approached the sled and found a competing musher in the sled bag. He had extensive, soft-ball-sized frostbite on his face and was undoubtedly hypothermic. His dogs were bedded on the trail. Running into such an extremely unforgiving storm with minimal trail distinction was overwhelming and confusing. I offered to help them get started so he could follow me. The musher got his team to their feet, but we had to attach a line from my team to his to start them moving.

We ran until it was dark. I could no longer see trail markers. The blizzard was worse and shining a headlight into blowing snow was further blinding. We stopped. To avoid getting separated from the team, I took the parachute cord I always pack in my sled, extended about 100 feet of it, tied one end of it to my sled and the other to my wrist, then made a circle looking for a trail marker. I did not find one. I guided my way to the other musher by walking directly next to his dogs while holding the gang-line. I stood within a foot of him and had to yell to be heard over the wind, "We're going have to spend the night right here. If we keep moving, we're really going to be lost!"

His split-second, emphatic response declared, "We're going to die."

I instantly realized as I looked at his swollen-eyed, frost-bitten face that he was beyond exhaustion and psychologically spent. I wanted to 'shake him up' so I got right in his face and said, "You might die, but I'm too f___ing stubborn!" I continued with insulting remarks to get him riled and mad, mad enough to fight--for his life! We fed the dogs, positioned them into a pile to share body heat, positioned our sleds as a windbreak for them, and spent the most miserable night on the ice during an epic blizzard. I crawled into my sleeping bag with my beaver mittens, my muck lucks, and arctic suit. I shivered until dawn. We later discovered the officials in Koyuk knew we were stranded, but discontinued rescue efforts to avoid jeopardizing the safety of the rescuers due to violence of the storm.

The storm raged the entire night. A welcomed light of the morning stirred us as we fed and tended the dogs, found the trail, and continued. Gladstone led my team with the other musher and his team following us. Gladstone was truly magnificent. I am convinced that incredible dog watched for the trail markers because if we were 10 or 20 feet from the marker, he would independently steer us back to the trail. Noteworthy, the wind was forcibly piercing to our faces, the trail was under snow and drifts, and the dogs were, at times, shoulder deep wallowing in snow. Gladstone busted through all of it while pulling the team behind him. For many miles, I kept my mouth shut and 'gave him his head' as he led us off the ice and into Koyuk where we were immediately instructed by race officials to see the community health nurse. The other musher was in really bad shape; he scratched (withdrew from the race) at Koyuk.

I took care of the dogs then was met by the community health nurse who had been alerted by the race officials of the night's events and was concerned I was hypothermic. She demanded to take a core temperature, which involves a rectal thermometer. In short, I skirted death to find myself toe-to-toe with nurse adamant she was doing her job to assure my well-being. With my pants down and a probing nurse with a thermometer, that soon became one of my more embarrassing moments of my Iditarod career.

My dogs rested several hours at Koyuk then Gladstone led my team and me to the finish line a couple of days later to place in the top 20.

The 1991 Iditarod marked the worst conditions I have experienced while racing. To date, I reminisce that race, shudder with memories of that night, and marvel at Gladstone. Throughout the entire sea ice passage, Gladstone never offered to retaliate, quit, or relinquish his duties as a lead dog. Gladstone saved my life, another musher's life, and the lives of over 20 dogs that night and day while guiding us through the worst elements the Iditarod could provide. Gladstone never acknowledged a problem nor accepted any type of fanfare for his accomplishments. True to his constitution, he returned to Montana to assist harness-training puppies that spring, relaxed during the summer when it was too warm to run, then reported for fall-training the following September because a job needed to be done.

Tail 9: Bear

Lead dogs are very important dogs for any dog team, but wheel dogs also can be instrumentally important; wheel dogs are the dogs directly in front of the sled. Wheel dogs steer the sled so they need to be strong, steady, and agile. Good wheel dogs make driving the sled a great deal easier.

Bear was one of my best wheel dogs. As a puppy I gave Bear to a rancher, however Bear wore out his welcome when he started chasing the rancher's calves. Before long, the rancher returned him to me. Bear's homecoming marked a renewed residency with me. He started training and slowly meshed with my main racing team.

Bear was Oly's son, but more mellow than his dad. He was off-white with a slightly coarse hair coat, blocky-shaped and had muscle tone as hard as granite. His strength was a valued asset to steer my sled as a wheel dog.

Bear was stoic, yet yielded silent precocious tendencies—a funny dog. He liked affection and was good with kids. Ordinarily he was not a fighter, nor did he instigate fights, but when provoked, defended himself to the death. Bear was in one fight, which resulted in a tail and rectal injury. I amputated part of his tail. The rectal damage caused a chronic condition of dribbling. Yet, this handicap never extinguished his desire to work.

I raced a weekend in Wisconsin. For road trips I transport the dog in the "dog box," which is an enclosed topper on the bed of the truck that has individual kennels for the dogs. The dog box on my truck was full, so I arranged a roomy spot under the dog box with blankets for Bear. He jumped into the area and quickly curled into a ball to rest. The remainder of the area under the box was filled with my personal gear, harnesses for the dogs, plus miscellaneous items required for the race. Behind all of that, I packed 50-pounds of frozen, ground beaver meat inside a bag for the dogs.

Bear traveled well to Wisconsin. During a trip of that duration, I make frequent stops and allow the dogs to leave their kennels, stretch, and go to the bathroom. After each stop, Bear freely jumped into the spot I had prepared for him and nestled into his blankets to rest. During the night before the race, Bear discarded the charade of resting on blankets, and weaseled his way to the bagged beaver meat and ate over 10-pounds before the race!

The following day upon discovering the pillaged beaver meat cache, I decided I would run him anyway. Bear completed a 58-mile run, however, stopped about every mile or two to defecate, which was a huge delay. The two days thereafter, Bear performed wonderfully and we won the race.

The funniest thing I remember about Bear was when I was travelling home from Alaska after running the Iditarod. Again, I arranged a comfortable spot underneath the dog box. When we crossed the border from Alaska into Canada, I waited on the border approximately 20 to 30 minutes. No border guards presented themselves, even though there were two cars in front of mine.

The sign read, "Stay in your vehicle." So, I got out of the truck, walked to the station and looked in the windows. Although I saw no one, the border guards saw me because when I returned to my truck, a guard suddenly appeared and waved the first two cars in front of me across the border. The guard then approached my vehicle and requested a barrage of information from me, including, "Do you have a weapon?"

"No. I sent my weapon home," I truthfully responded. More guards appeared and they asked me three more times if I had a weapon and three more times I answered, "No."

I was informed they would be conducting a search of my vehicle. I was driving an extended cab pickup truck, which I was told to empty. I had a box of 22-caliber ammunition in the ashtray that I had not emptied from hunting season the previous autumn. The oversight created all kinds of excitement because I had not declared it. I defended, "You didn't ask the about ammunition. You asked if I had a weapon!"

The search of the cab produced nothing more of interest for the border officials; therefore, they soon informed me they would be searching underneath the dog box. One official dropped the tailgate and found himself staring nose to nose with Bear—big, brawny Bear. Bear was a sweetheart of a dog and would have never threatened anyone; but the border guard must have thought otherwise. The guard closed the tailgait, ended the search, and told me "go ahead." I got into the truck and chuckled because the guard did not act startled nor asked me to remove the dog. He simply ended the search.

Bear spent much of his career as a wheel dog. I was able to retire him into a pet home where he successfully integrated into family life and did not take up cattle herding nor rustling in his retirement.

Tail 10: Ranger

Ranger was a big red, rangy dog. Early in his career, he injured a back leg during a training accident and thereafter would occasionally limp slightly when he would first start running until he warmed up. Ranger was a hard-working dog that loved his job. He had boundless, yet contained, enthusiasm to run regardless of any physical malady. He never ran lead and was usually in the wheel position. Ranger had a warm personality. His ability was less that of many of his teammates; however, he overcame any physical inferiority with his fantastic attitude.

Ranger went with me to the John Beargrease Race. I took a 12-hour layover at the Sky Port checkpoint after the team hauled a dog, Red, into Sky Port. Red was a young dog and had gotten tired en route to Sky Port. I intended to take my 12-hour layover and drop Red from my team — meaning leave the dog with the veterinary team until my handler was able to assume care while I continued racing.

Dr. Charlie Berger, a trusted friend and colleague of mine with a vivacious personality, was the veterinarian working the Sky Port checkpoint. After 12 hours of rest, Ranger had stiffened up, which was pretty typical until he warmed up again. Charlie did not like to see Ranger limping, or any other dog for that matter; meanwhile, Red, the dog I planned to drop at that checkpoint was screaming to go. Charlie urged with a Northeastern accent, "C'mon, give the young dog a chance." Against my better judgment I dropped Ranger out of the team and allowed Red to run. Red's enthusiasm lasted for about eight miles out of the checkpoint. We had to haul Red in the sled for the next 60 miles to the Grand Portage checkpoint. I wish I had taken Ranger, and I still love to tease Charlie about it.

I took Ranger to the Iditarod that same spring. I had no one to ride to Alaska with me. The trip was 2,500 miles from my home and required 52 hours of continuous driving. I was talking to a treasured friend of mine, Jack Beckstrom, who was a harness and sled maker from Olney, MT. Jack said he had a person working for him that would like go to Alaska and could probably ride with me. Jack gave me the man's contact information. The remainder of this story is disparaging at times, so I will refer to the man as Joe Handler. I called Joe and he ardently wanted to go.

Joe informed me he had worked for Frank Teasley, a musher and friend of mine from Wyoming, and asserted he was "a good hand with dogs." Joe continued that he had worked at several ranches. Right there should have been an indication to me there could be a problem; because if a ranch gets a good hand, they try to keep them.

I agreed to take Joe to Alaska with the stipulation that I would NOT pay him a wage, but I would pay for his expenses. We further agreed that I had a place for him to stay when we arrived to Alaska. In turn, he would provide care for any dogs I may have to 'drop' while I was on the race. I concluded our discussion by saying, "Let's pack light because I don't have a whole lot of room in the truck with my dogs. Bring a duffel bag and maybe a backpack and call it good."

Within two days of the conversation, Joe presented with a backpack, a big duffel bag, a large bedroll, a 30/30 rifle and a pair of snowshoes. We had a brief discussion over the excess equipment that he brought and the issues regarding border-crossing with a weapon. I made him leave some of his belongings; we did not have room.

We got into the truck and started north with the dogs. Within moments, Joe announced he expected payment for traveling with me. I said, "Look, there's no money involved here. I told you I'd take care of all the expenses." The refusal released an outpouring of reasons why he needed payment despite the previously arranged agreement: he had so many kids, he just quit a job, he was hurt because of riding bucking horses…. the list continued.

A deal is a deal and I replied, "no." Joe pouted well past the Canadian border.

The disparity of our communication worsened as the trip progressed. From the initial conversation I had with Joe, he had professed he was "a good hand with dogs." His actions proved otherwise. I was beyond delighted to arrive in Alaska after our travel together for three days.

We went to the mushers meeting in Anchorage. My friend, Frank Teasley, was on the opposite side of the convention meeting room and saw me enter with Joe. Instead of receiving Frank's customary welcome, Frank gave me a nod of his head to insinuate we needed to talk. Frank greeted me unusually--not a "hi" or "hello," but rather a scolding question, "What's he doing here with you?"

"Frank," I defended, "he told me he used to work for you!"

Frank quickly replied, "But did he tell you I fired him?"

How clear it suddenly became.

I took 17 dogs to Alaska and ran all 17 of them in the ceremonial start of the Iditarod race. At the restart in Wasilla, I wanted some of my veterinary friends to assess Ranger. Ranger never presented with any obvious injury; however, it was an opportunity to access several, exceptional veterinarians. Seven veterinarians examined Ranger; Dr. Dominic Grandjean, a friend of mine from France, was the veterinarian that really spent a lot of time tracing each of Ranger's gastrocnemius muscles all the way to the tendons. Dominic concluded that the right gastrocnemius tendon was slightly enlarged compared to the left. I decided to leave Ranger out of the Iditarod race and run 16 dogs. Note: I took 16 all of the way to White Mountain, which is 77 miles from the finish line, and dropped one dog. I finished with 15 dogs that year.

My decision allocated Joe to care for one dog, Ranger. I started the race and traveled several miles down the trail with a wonderfully moving dog team. During that time, Ranger excused himself from Joe's care and bolted to the trail in search of me. I was quite alarmed when I first recognized Ranger coming from behind; we were almost 30 miles down the trail. Ranger recognized me immediately. After all, Ranger passed other teams who were not me and continued running. I said, "Come on, boy." He passed my sled, filed in behind the other dogs, and ran to the next checkpoint where I delivered him to an Iditarod volunteer to care for him.

To this day, Frank likes to tell the story about how I got to Skwentna, a distance over 100 miles from the restart, and Ranger was following along behind my team. Actually, it was not that far into the race. However, Frank teases me that I provided transportation to Alaska for Joe plus room and board for nearly a month; and in return, the man failed to be responsible for one dog.

I am not sure if Ranger followed me because he wanted to race or he feared the incompetence of Joe. I am certain that Ranger was missed during the race. He had a hearty and cheerful demeanor that was an integral part of any team.

Tail 11: Amigo

Amigo is the epitome of a mushing dog. He is a big, brawny, 65-pound male whose presence is radiantly joyful. He is also as hard-working and versatile as any dog a musher could imagine. Amigo reminds me of Oly minus any malice or aggression. Solid and compact with a cream-colored wiry coat, his round face always dons a smile; and he has pigment missing on his left eye. His tail is in constant motion. He was born from a litter with the theme of calendar months: May, June, July, Aug, Gus, and Amigo--my grand-daughter thought he looked like "Amigo." He and his littermates have beautiful conformation.

Amigo will run anywhere on the team. He will run on the right or the left of gang-line, next to an intact male without issue. He also runs in lead, but usually at a slower pace. Or at wheel, which is where I love to have his strength and steadiness. My preference is to run him at wheel next to his brother, Gus. They are matched well physically and synergistically.

A couple of years ago, I was doing a short training run on a four-wheeler near the kennel with an eight-dog team. There was not enough snow for sleds, so we hooked the gang-line to the four-wheeler for dry-land training. I asked my kennel partner to ride on the four-wheeler with me; because we had recently had some drifting snow and windy conditions. I commanded the dogs to go off-trail and cross a small ditch so we could do some gee-haw training in a field. From the trail, I did not see the three-foot snow berm that had drifted on the up-side of the ditch. The dogs traversed it, but the four-wheeler jammed into the drift with snow teeming over the front of it as we drove into the embankment. We were abruptly stopped. My kennel partner went behind the four-wheeler and tried to push as we called up the dogs to pull while I worked the throttle. The four-wheeler barely budged.

At one another's side, Amigo and Gus went to work. In unison, the two dogs leaned their bodies into their harnesses and maximized every muscle to pull us free. With each inch we gained, I reinforced their efforts with praise. The boys continued to party with barks and thrusts as their flexed bodies dug and ripped at the snow beneath them. After directly pulling with their heads low and leaning, they would release and rise slightly, then slam their power into the harness attached to the tug lines trying to get momentum. The muscles in their shoulders, backs, and thighs rippled through their thick coats as they worked. With every word of praise I gave them, they began to yell back at me and each other like, "Let's get this done!" Their energy flowed into the gang-line and the other dogs soon got into the rhythm. The other dogs reached with their arms and shoulders to the snow-covered ground ahead of them and used the bulging muscles in their rear legs to push their backs into the harnesses to leverage power. After several succinct attempts at the request of my command, the team soon jerked us from the quagmire. The area of the snow where we passed looked like bulls had rutted there.

We called "whoa" and walked up the line laughing at the dogs' responses. All were breathing with heaving chests. Their tails were wagging and some had their bodies swaying with muzzles stretched in the air singing "woowoowoo" to us. They knew they had done a good job pulling and were having fun all the while.

That outing was not days of running an arctic ultra-marathon, nor any heroic passage through perilous trail conditions. It was a leisurely run training excursion with an obstacle that allowed those dogs to purposefully give 100%, if only for a few minutes. Simply beautiful. This is what our dogs were bred and born to do.

Conclusion

Although there are additional races I would like to have entered and certainly races I would like to have won, I am not disappointed. The dogs have taken me places I could never have imagined and I am thankful. I have a terrific bunch of dogs, and I love what I do. With advancing age and its unwanted impediments, I continue to maintain a kennel, train dogs, and participate when I can in whatever capacity I am able. Although I do not have an office practice, I maintain my veterinary medical license and belong to professional organizations to continue learning. The decades spent with dogs have seen many trends come and go, but I believe more and better practices have prevailed surrounding sled dog and dog-powered events. My hope is the Iditarod will be run for many years to come and the evolving knowledge will amass to propel veterinary science, as well as complimentary practices. The dogs, however, are basically the same—the most amazing of animals. I feel blessed to have been part of the experience called the Iditarod.

---

[13] Photographer unlisted (1993.) The Last Great Race. Frontiersman Iditarod Edition, P. 1.

Authors

Terry Adkins, DVM enjoys his life with dogs, gardening, garage sales, and big-game hunting. He is an avid reader and has wanted to author a book for decades. He is pictured with one of his treasured lead-dogs, Irena, who is one of the smartest dogs he has ever had the privilege to train.

Jean Wise is a registered nurse and partnered with Terry in 2008. She enjoys hiking, camping, and gardening. She has raced recreationally and appreciates the dedication of the professional mushers, however, has never aspired to race the Iditarod. She loves to train and develop dogs. She oversees much of their kennel management and implemented research projects to enhance the well-being of their dogs.

www.ingramcontent.com/pod-product-compliance
Lightning Source LLC
LaVergne TN
LVHW051655080426
835511LV00017B/2578